M000200849

the BINGE WATCHER'S guide

THE HANDMAID'S TALE

USA TODAY BESTSELLING AUTHOR
Jamie K. Schmidt

The Binge Watcher's Guide to the Handmaid's Tale: An Unofficial Companion
© Jamie K. Schmidt 2020

All Rights Reserved. No part of this book may be reproduced or transmitted in any form or by any means, electronic or mechanical, including photocopying, without permission in writing from the publisher.

The Binge Watcher's Guide is a Trademark of Riverdale Avenue Books

For more information contact:
Riverdale Avenue Books
5676 Riverdale Avenue
Riverdale, NY 10471.

www.riverdaleavebooks.com
Design by www.formatting4U.com
Cover by Scott Carpenter

Digital ISBN: 9781626015708
Trade Paperback ISBN: 9781626015715
Hardback ISBN: 9781626015722

First Edition, November 2020

Acknowledgements

I wanted to thank Margaret Atwood for engaging my young mind and expanding my world. Also my thanks for the vision of the television show creator Bruce Miller, and the executive producers Daniel Wilson, Fran Sears and Warren Littlefield. Kudos to Reed Morano, the director of the Hulu series and Colin Watkinson's excellent cinematography for their well-deserved awards.

Table of Contents

Acknowledgements 3
Table of Contents 5
Introduction...For Evil to Thrive, Good People Just Have to Do Nothing ... 1
How to Use This Book and What to Expect 7
Season One
    Chapter One: Hang on to Your Wings, It's Going to Be a Bumpy Ride . 13
    Chapter Two: It's My Party and I'll Cry if I Want To 19
    Chapter Three: Buckle up, Buttercups................................... 23
    Chapter Four: This Shit is Contagious 27
    Chapter Five: Hypocrite Thy Name is Gilead 31
    Chapter Six: A Place of One's Own...................................... 35
    Chapter Seven: Use the Force, Luke 39
    Chapter Eight: Waterford Thy Name is Douche 41
    Chapter Nine: Praised Be, Bitch.. 45
    Chapter Ten: Terror Tastes Like Gun Metal 49
    Season One Reflections 55
Season Two
    Chapter Eleven: Take Me Out to the Ballgame........................ 59
    Chapter Twelve: Revenge is a Dish Served Cold...................... 63
    Chapter Thirteen: Blessed Be the Fruit Loops 67
    Chapter Fourteen: June vs. Offred.. 71
    Chapter Fifteen: It's a Nice Day for a White Wedding 77
    Chapter Sixteen: Breakfast at Tiffany's 81
    Chapter Seventeen: Offorfuckssake 85
    Chapter Eighteen: Back in the Closet.................................... 89
    Chapter Nineteen: Aloha Treason and Coconuts...................... 95
    Chapter Twenty: It Gets Worse— a Crescendo of Suffering........... 101
    Chapter Twenty-One: I Went For A Drive and Never Went Back .. 107

Chapter Twenty-Two: Mommy Dearest 111
Chapter Twenty-Three: Get in the Fucking Van, June.................... 115
Season Two Reflections 121
Season Three
Chapter Twenty-Four: Burning Down the House 127
Chapter Twenty-Five: Give 'Em the Old Razzle Dazzle 131
Chapter Twenty-Six: Snark and Banter.. 137
Chapter Twenty-Seven: The Beatings Will Continue 143
Chapter Twenty-Eight: What about Hannah? 149
Chapter Twenty-Nine: Tell Me How You Really Feel, June 153
Chapter Thirty: Alice Down the Rabbit Hole.................................. 157
Chapter Thirty-One: No More Fucks to Give 161
Chapter Thirty-Two: Do You Know What That's Worth? 165
Chapter Thirty-Three: What Has This Season Has Been Lacking? . 171
Chapter Thirty-Four: Karma is Only a Bitch if You Are 179
Chapter Thirty-Five: Oh What a Tangled Web We Weave 185
Chapter Thirty-Six: Under His Fucking Eye................................... 191
After You've Watched.. 195
Bibliography 198
About the Author 199
Other Riverdale Avenue Books You Might Like 200

Season One

Introduction

For Evil to Thrive, Good People Just Have to Do Nothing

"But who can remember pain, once it's over?
All that remains of it is a shadow, not in the mind even, in the flesh.
Pain marks you, but too deep to see. Out of sight, out of mind."
~ *Margaret Atwood, The Handmaid's Tale*

My first experience with *The Handmaid's Tale* by Margaret Atwood was when I was 16 years old in 1986. The book had been nominated for the Nebula Award that year, an award that's given out by the Science Fiction and Fantasy Writers of America (SFWA), and since I was an aspiring science fiction/fantasy novelist, I wanted to read all the Nebula entries to see what the magic ticket was to get a publishing contract.

As a sheltered white, cis, het teenager blinded by her privilege at the time, most of the book's message went over my head and I remember being pissed at the ending... I thought it was a bullshit cop out of an ending. If I had tried that... instant rejection from the editors. The only thing that saved it from being a wall banger—a book that you throw against the wall—was that I did get a message that resonated with me for most of my life:

For evil to thrive, good people just have to do nothing.

It wasn't enough for good people just to hope that the problem would go away. The good people had to rise up and take a stand, even when it was painful or inconvenient or unpopular to be silent and complacent.

But the ending still bothered me. So I decided that Nick had sent the protagonist to freedom instead of death or punishment. The thing is, I looked for romance in everything I read. In some ways, I still do.

I thought back then, what kind of a stupid book would have a

1

shitty ending like that, where he would just give her up to the Eye for execution? To quote the kid from *The Princess Bride* movie, "Jesus, Grandpa, why did you read me this thing for?"

Oh, my sweet summer child. Past Jamie had a lot to learn about the real world. I had a lot to learn about writing as well, that not every story has a happily ever after, and that sometimes the greatest romance the heroine has is learning to love herself.

After that, I mostly forgot about the book. It had made me uncomfortable and the dystopian society seemed so implausible and more like something that happened in the past. That shit was so 1800's. Women had the right to vote. We had fought for equal rights. The hard part was over, right?

Did I mention I was a very sheltered and privileged 16 year-old cis het girl?

Flash forward five years. I'm now 21 and the 1990 Volker Schlondorff movie is on HBO. I vaguely remembered the details of the book at this point, but I was so excited to see the movie. Finally, I'd find out what the handmaid's fate was! There was no way that Hollywood would let this remain vague.

... I don't remember a lot from the movie. Looking back on it now, it was very 80s inspired. Natasha Richardson was gorgeous as Kate, the former librarian. Those details weren't from the book, but it was nice to have a name for her other than Offred. And Aidan Quinn was Nick. Hubba hubba. He was so fine. Robert Duvall and Faye Dunaway, as the commander and his wife, were perfectly sadistic, but I don't remember Elizabeth McGovern as Moira at all. I remember thinking at the time that Robert Duvall was a disgusting old man. Not the commander, but Robert Duvall. That's how good of an actor he was. It wasn't until 2003 in *Secondhand Lions* that I appreciated this. All of his other roles from 1990 until 2003, I saw the commander instead of whatever character Robert was portraying. He turned my stomach. Fortunately, Hub from Secondhand Lions is now how I see Robert Duvall. It's much nicer this way.

And yet, I still didn't get the impact of the movie or book's message.

All I got out of the movie was the answer to my question about what happened to the handmaid. I wanted a happy ending. The commander gets what's coming to him. Serena Joy is husband-less, and therefore powerless. Kate and Nick's "romance" was validated. What I thought was wildly romantic back in the early 90s, was bordering on creepy when I recently re-watched the movie. Nick kisses her out of the blue, and yanks her nightgown down for their first "romantic" encounter. Yuck.

But in the movie, Nick was working undercover for Mayday—the resistance—all along. He got her and their baby out to the "mountains" for safety. And like the 1984 movie, *Against All Odds,* I knew the two lovers would eventually find each other again. And since Nick was such a mensch, he'd also bring Kate's daughter back to her, who was pretty much an afterthought for the entire movie.

And what about Gilead? Back in the 90s, it was a laughable concept in my sheltered world. A dystopian country whose politics were as real to me at Frank Herbert's *Dune.* I had more of a chance of becoming a Bene Gesserit than a Handmaid, even though at the time if Gilead happened it would be me on the bed in a red dress.

Flash forward 26 years, and Hulu has made a series out of Margaret Atwood's book. I'm now 47 years old. Too old to be a handmaid. Not rich and powerful enough to be a Commander's wife. Not domestically talented to be a Martha. And without the temperament to be an Econowife. I'd strictly be an Unwoman—if I wasn't executed during the purge.

In 2017, Gilead is no longer a dystopian fantasy. It's a believable outcome that doesn't have to wait for a nuclear disaster or a civil war to happen. It's practically a few laws away. I'm now a mother and Gilead looms closer every day. The idea that someone could take my child away to give to another "worthier" family isn't fucking fantasy anymore. Trump was the president. States are passing bills that reduce pregnant women to incubators. People are showing their ugly sides.

Nolite te bastardes carborundorum indeed.

Not to mention that at the time this guide was written, we were at the height of the COVID-19 pandemic, and race riots for the unjust killing of black men and women were commonplace. Martial law and Trump dissolving the constitution to "better protect America's interests" seemed only a Twitter rant away.

Shit has gotten real.

I finally got it. I finally got the meaning in the 1985 book, why it was nominated for a Nebula Award, and why it has haunted me, both consciously and sub-consciously, for over 30 years.

The world that Margaret Atwood has created is terrifying. Show runner Bruce Miller keeps true to the spirit of the book, while holding up a mirror to modern society. The actors are gritty and real. And the series itself feels like a documentary instead of fiction, as if Gilead is only a border away from sanity.

I had thought I was prepared for the series. I was even looking forward to it... hoping, at last, for a conclusive ending. I wanted a happy ending for Nick and "Kate" and her first daughter. Except in the Hulu series, Kate is June, and her husband is very much alive. And as I'm watching, I'm experiencing June's story as if I was June. It didn't matter that I am long past my childbearing prime. I was with June from the moment they snatched her daughter away from her. Because I could see Gilead happening. Right now. Tomorrow. All it would take for evil to flourish would be good people to do nothing.

Good people stayed home from the polls, and look who got elected President in 2016.

In 2020, we're still not out of the woods. I'm not exhaling until February 1st 2021—at least. And even then, we can't let down our guard. We've got Ofdonald on the Supreme Court, who bears more than a passing resemblance to how I've always pictured Serena Joy.

Amy Coney Barrett is a part of a religious group called People of Praise, which surprisingly enough, was not one of Margaret Atwood's inspirations for the Sons of Jacob. But it is ultra-conservative Catholic-esque, and as the *New York Times* reported, "Until recently, the group used the term "handmaids" to refer to female leaders, inspired by a Biblical reference to Mary, the mother of Jesus, as "the handmaid of the Lord." They shifted to "women leader" when the popular TV adaptation of the book "The Handmaid's Tale" gave the term a sinister cast." (Graham and LaFraniere, 2020)

If it quacks like a duck and walks like a duck...

Before Ofdonald was sworn in, stepping on Ruth Bader Ginsburg's shroud, back when the horrors of the Trump presidency were still in their infancy, I binge watched the first season of *The Handmaid's Tale*. I didn't mean to and I probably shouldn't have, but I did. I watched it alone because my husband wasn't interested and I watched it in the dark, at night, because I couldn't move to turn on the light once the show began.

I refused to go to bed that night until I saw some hope, some light in the very dark tunnel that is the first season. Every episode felt like a gut shot to me. I waited to become numb. I waited to see justice. I waited to stop sobbing, great gulping tears of agony because I was terrified I was looking at the future. There was no way I could go to sleep without seeing a crack of hope, because what if I woke up and Guardians were at my door, taking my son away from me?

Elisabeth Moss, the actress that plays the titular handmaid, June, even recommended not to binge watch it because each episode packs quite a punch, and people needed the time to think about the message and process it. Margaret Atwood agreed that, "It's very emotionally fraught." (Lawler, 2017)

This book, though, is for the binge watchers. The ones who want to be so engrossed in the narrative that they feel they are wearing the red dress that is smothering them. It's also for the people who watch horror movies with one hand over their eyes so they don't see the gory or frightening bits, and it's for the people that read the ending of a book first so they know what to expect and can prepare for it. And lastly it's for the people who watched *The Handmaid's Tale* and want someone to help process all the feelings the show invoked.

This is the book I wish I had had as a companion while I watched episode after episode alone and in the dark. Something to tether me to hope and a reassurance that we are not in Gilead. Not yet. And if we act now, we can stop it.

How to Use This Book and What to Expect

"Gilead is a city of them that work iniquity,
and is polluted with blood."
~ Hosea 6:8, King James Bible

In the following chapters, there will be trigger warnings and a little levity to take away from the wretched world on the screen—the one that is currently so close to the world outside. Each chapter in this book correlates to an episode from Season One through Season Three. At the start of each chapter, I'll post a trigger warning for what to expect and a gut punch meter to prepare you for the horrors you're about to bear witness to.

Your mileage may vary. Going through the trigger warnings, almost every episode has one for rape. You should know that upfront. Because even when June is giving in to the commander at Jezebels, or even Nick for the first time, it's still rape. The only ones having consensual sex are Fred and Serena, and that's somehow *verboten* because they're not having sex for procreation.

Gilead doesn't make a lot of sense. But since when did sexism and racism make sense?

And at the end of each chapter, I'll suggest some self-care things to help you get through. By the way, here's your first trigger warning: This book has tons of swearing in it. And this show is a violent, gruesome story about raping women and taking away their children. So buckle up.

Also, I am not a doctor or a therapist or even remotely trained in helping someone with trauma, so please don't let my self-care and trigger warnings stop you from seeking professional assistance if you need it. What triggers me and what I think is a gut punch could be massively different from your experiences. Treat yourself well and be kind to yourself.

7

There are some chapters that have rape in them that I've marked with a low gut punch rating. On a scale of one to five, I might mark it as a two. That's not because I think rape is not horrifying or worthy of a gut punch, but because the scene could be much worse. There are rape scenes that are a five and I've marked them that way.

In my opinion, the hardest episodes to watch are:

- Season One, Episode Three: Late
- Season One, Episode Eight: Jezebels
- Season One, Episode Ten: Night

Season One is a motherfucker. If you can survive the first season, it doesn't get much better, but you become numb and inured to the horrors of Gilead. Still, these later episodes are also rough:

- Season Two, Episode Two: Unwomen
- Season Three, Episode Nine: Heroic

Take special care when watching these five episodes.

Beware, that there are spoilers for the show as well. The chapters will discuss what happened in each episode along with what I was thinking and feeling during the action.

It's helpful, but not required, to have seen the movie and have read the book. They all mix in together in my memories.

And just so we're all on the same page…

Margaret Atwood wrote the book *The Handmaid's Tale*. It was published in 1985.

In 1990 it was made into a movie directed by Volker Schlöndorff, screenplay by Harold Pinter, and starred:

- Natasha Richardson as Kate (June/The Handmaid)
- Faye Dunaway as Serena Joy
- Aidan Quinn as Nick
- Elizabeth McGovern as Moira
- Victoria Tennant as Aunt Lydia
- Robert Duvall as The Commander
- Blanche Baker as Ofglen
- Traci Lind as Ofwarren / Janine

It's a very white cast, and the movie has a distinct 80s sci-fi feel to it that's reflected in the outfits and hairstyles to a distracting degree. It also tries to give a half-assed happy ending that is not very satisfying and still leaves unanswered questions.

At the very start of the movie we see all the black people being herded into trucks and containers and shipped off somewhere. Maybe the colonies? We don't really know. In the book, they were the Children of Ham who were at best relocated to reservations or the colonies, but most likely murdered.

Strangely enough it's the movie's vagueness of the details that keep Gilead in the fictional realm for me. It stays true to Atwood's book, for the most part. The handmaids and Marthas are very much living what female black slaves endured, which Atwood appropriated and that doesn't sit well with me. The TV show does a better job of telling a multi-cultural story, but that makes it all the more horrifying and real than the movie. However, the TV show also has a tendency to "fridge" black handmaids to show June's (a white woman) pain. Fridging is a term mostly used in comic books when the female love interest is killed to further the male hero's plot. Comic book writer Gail Simone came up with the term in 1999, after Green Lantern's girlfriend Alexandra DeWitt was murdered and stuffed into a literal refrigerator. (Grady, 2019)

The liberties the movie takes to depart from the book doesn't distract from the story, however. And for the one hour and 48 minutes it runs, it hits all the highlights with the following ending that's pure 80s movie magic: Kate the handmaid kills the commander and her Eye lover gets her out to the mountains to have their baby in solitude.

But what about Kate's first child?

Oh yeah… the movie pretty much forgot about her. That also puts it more in the realm of fantasy for me. I couldn't relate with a character that forgot about her own child or gave her up without a fight, which Kate pretty much did.

Part of what makes the Hulu show so terrifying is that it expands on the concepts in Atwood's book and allows you to learn more about the characters and their motivations. The nuances of everyone's life prior to Gilead are fascinating to watch and it's frightening to see the plots that lead up to Gilead because it could so easily happen.

In 2017, Hulu started the television series with the following cast:

9

- Elisabeth Moss as June
- Yvonne Strahovski as Serena Joy
- Joseph Fiennes as Fred Waterford
- Ann Dowd as Aunt Lydia
- Amanda Brugel as Rita (the Waterford's Martha)
- Madeline Brewer as Janine
- Max Minghella as Nick
- O-T Fagbenle as Luke
- Samira Wiley as Moira

This is a much more diverse cast, which adds to the realism of the series—with one weird exception. Racism doesn't seem to exist in Hulu's Gilead as much as it does in Trump's America. It's there, of course, but no one mentions June's mixed race marriage—just that it was invalid because Gilead doesn't believe in divorce. One of the commanders is black and apparently fertile! Which must really chap the sterile old white guys' asses.

It makes me wonder how did Hulu's fictional America become so enlightened to reducing racism and still wind up as a country like Gilead? You would think the commanders would be white supremacists too. They were in the book and in the movie.

The comparatively small amount of racism in Gilead is the only thing that keeps the Hulu TV show in the fantasy realm for me. Which is really fucked up when you think about it. And I try not to think what a Trump/Pence Gilead would look like. I hope I never have to experience it firsthand.

"We lived, as usual by ignoring. Ignoring
isn't the same as ignorance,
you have to work at it."
~ Margaret Atwood, The Handmaid's Tale

SEASON ONE

Chapter One: Hang on to Your Wings, It's Going to Be a Bumpy Ride

Season One, Episode One: Offred

"We thought we had such problems.
How were we to know we were happy?"
~ Margaret Atwood, The Handmaid's Tale

Trigger Warnings: Child abduction, women being beaten, hanging, rape.
Gut Punch Rating: 2 out of 5, unless you're unfamiliar with the story then 4.
Scariest Line: "This will all become ordinary." As the show goes on, you get a little numb to the everyday horror of Gilead.

Reminder, here there be spoilers...

The first episode opens up with a bang—a literal car crash and then a chase. Gunshots. And men with rifles stalking our heroine and her little girl. For a moment, we have hope that maybe the woman and her child will get away from the men after her... but she runs too soon and is captured, beaten unconscious, and her child taken from her.

It's a great opening scene because you're immediately engaged.

We next see her dressed as a handmaid in the iconic red dress with white wings on her head. Light is shining through the window, illuminating her like a bird in a cage, A contrast between the sunshine on the outside to the sunshine she had been running for her freedom under. Immediately, she talks about suicide and how things that were normal, are forbidden. She is now Offred, but used to be June Osborne, a married woman who had been trying to escape Gilead to Canada. She's played by Elisabeth Moss and the camera angles are upclose and personal to let the audience see every emotion flitting across her face.

13

Handmaid Lore: The girls are stripped of their names and are only referred to as belonging to their respective commander. In this case, Offred is literally Of Fred Waterford, a high-ranking commander of the Gilead forces.

Then we meet Serena Joy Waterford. Yvonne Strahovski oozes contempt and power. Dressed smartly in her teal blue suit, she isn't Faye Dunaway's Serena Joy, who was more of a caricature than a real character. Yvonne's Serena Joy is immediately someone who is a dangerous adversary, to the point when Commander Waterford walks in, she overshadows him as the villain.

Joseph Fiennes is more Will Shakespeare to me than any other character he's played in the past, and seems almost harmless in comparison. He is more polite than his wife, who had moments before compared the last handmaid to a stupid dog. He even seems disappointed when Offred behaves like a perfect handmaid—until she doesn't.

"You too," our heroine says after the commander tells her to have a nice day.

Just two words, but they're enough to stop him in his tracks and put Serena on high alert. Serena threatens Offred that if she gets trouble, she'll give trouble back. And after warning her that her marriage to the commander is until death parts them, she leaves.

Handmaid Lore: Gilead is a society of ranking. The males rank in order: Commanders of the Faithful, Angels (soldiers), and Guardians (peacekeepers, bodyguards, servants). And then there are the Eyes of God (The Eyes) who are Gilead's secret police. The men are the makers of rules, war, and politics. Females aren't a part of that, but they do have societal power and are also ranked. The Wives wear teal blue. The Aunts train the handmaids and they are dressed all in brown. The Handmaids wear red. The Marthas (servants) wear light greenish smocks, and the Econowives (wives of the guardians) wear gray.

The world building of the show is told through flashbacks and point of view shifts. In this episode, we see June's life before being captured, and her time in training at the Rachel and Leah Center (The Red Center) under Aunt Lydia. We see that she is partnered with Ofglen who she calls a "pious little shit." And we see her old friend Moira, who in present time, Offred mentions is glad she's not hanging on the wall. Some little hope that the handmaids can escape?

But then we meet Janine, back when they all first arrived at The Red Center. Janine had proudly told the Aunts to go fuck themselves and lost an eye because of it. As Moira tells June, "You don't need to have an eye to be breeding stock." Janine is then put into a circle of slut shaming, where the other handmaids are slapped if they don't tell her it was her fault she was raped, that she led the boys on. The handmaids are encouraged to shout, "Teach her a lesson." Escape doesn't seem possible. The level of brainwashing the Aunts are doing is insidious.

Easter Egg: The Aunt that slaps June in the back of the head for not saying, "Her fault" is Margaret Atwood.

I like this Offred over the book and movie version. I like hearing her thoughts and how she's not accepting this new life. She's enduring it until—as she and Moira pinky swore—they could get out of this and find her daughter Hannah.

Then, it's time for the rape ceremony.

We are told by Aunt Lydia that there was a plague of infertility followed by massive radiation, assumedly from a nuclear attack. So the commanders are allowed to rape the handmaids to get them pregnant. But it's all "okay" because the wife is right there while the rape is going on. It's a biblical thing.

"And when Rachel saw that she bare Jacob no children, Rachel envied her sister; and said unto Jacob, Give me children, or else I die. And Jacob's anger was kindled against Rachel: and he said, Am I in God's stead, who hath withheld from thee the fruit of the womb? And she said, Behold my maid Bilhah, go in unto her; and she shall bear upon my knees, that I may also have children by her. And she gave him Bilhah her handmaid to wife: and Jacob went in unto her. And Bilhah conceived, and bare Jacob a son." (James, 2020) (King James Bible Genesis 30:1)

After an eternity of watching Fred rape June with Serena watching on expressionless, it's over. June's haunted eyes say more about the epic amount of shit wrong with this idea than Serena's cold "Get out." June goes outside in desperation, whether it's to get some air or escape or to look at the moon, which is the only thing that she says hasn't changed. And Nick sees her, shooing her back inside before anyone else catches her. Nick is the Waterford's driver. He's not as sexy as Aidan Quinn, but I can see the connection between them. Though, he has more time in a series, rather than a two-hour movie, to develop a relationship with June.

Whether it was losing an eye, or being slut shamed, or if she's just started drinking The Red Center Kool-Aid, Janine has gone crazy. She has gone bye-bye, talking to the other handmaids like she is their waitress, unnerving the other handmaids. Alma tells her to knock it off, because she doesn't want extra prayers, while Moira cracks Janine one across the face to snap her out of it. And Moira warns June that if Janine does that again, to smack some sense into her, "because that shit is catching."

The narrative then flips back into the present. Nick didn't tell anyone that June was outside and she wonders if he is someone to trust.

This is followed by another ceremony, one called a "Particution" for being a cross between participation and execution. Gilead loves its ceremonies and you can thank Commander Waterford for coming up with that little gem.

Aunt Lydia displays a man who is accused of raping a handmaid and killing an unborn baby in the process. She encourages the handmaids to form a circle and give the rapist his punishment. Now, let's be clear. He's not being punished for rape. No one gives a shit about that. He's being punished because a baby, who is sacred to Gilead, has died.

The handmaids are allowed off their leashes to participate in the rapist/baby murderer's punishing. And all their rage is allowed in between whistle blows. Janine smiles benignly on, rubbing her pregnant stomach with a blissful expression on her face, as the handmaids rip the man apart. Janine is still batshit crazy and, prior to the ceremony, dropped the bomb on June that Moira is dead.

It turns out though, that the "rapist" was a member of a resistance. Ofglen and June bond a bit, each surprised that the other isn't a "pious little shit."

"They do that really well, making us distrust them," Oflgen says.

She warns June that there's a spy (an Eye) in her house. June wonders who, as she hides from Serena.

Up in her room, June feels a little bit of hope. She's found friends in Ofglen and Nick, and she's beginning to think that this Gilead thing may be temporary, that she can endure it for Hannah's sake. The episode ends with her saying to herself, "My name is June."

And then come the credits with the song, "You Don't Own Me" by Lesley Gore.

Self-Care Suggestion:

Keep the feeling that June is going to kick some ass and we're going to be right there with her. Grab a blanket, a glass of your favorite beverage and some popcorn. Bring on episode 2.

Chapter Two: It's My Party and I'll Cry if I Want To

Season One, Episode Two: Birthday

"As all historians know, the past is a great darkness,
and filled with echoes."
~ *Margaret Atwood, The Handmaid's Tale*

Trigger Warnings: Rape, baby being taken from his mother
Gut Punch Rating: 2

The episode starts off with June and Ofglen on their way back from the market, when suddenly they see a man being taken by the Eye. Ofglen tells June about the network, an "us" that's fighting back. Through her, we start to find out more about the world, like that St. Patrick's Cathedral in NYC was blown up, the rocks scattered into the Hudson. We also learn that the capital of Gilead is in Alaska and the flag has only two stars.

Back home, Nick warns June not to get too close to Ofglen and that the Commander wants to see her alone in his study that night. Something which is forbidden. As June puts it, "We're two legged wombs, not concubines."

The Birth Mobile arrives—a red van that picks up all the handmaids to bring them to the homes where other handmaids are giving birth. Turns out the chances of a healthy birth are one in five these days.

Janine is the one giving birth this time, causing June to flash back to when she gave birth to Hannah. While Janine is doing the hard work, the wives put on a pantomime about giving birth. Each wife pretends she is pregnant while all her blue-dressed friends surround her and offer their support. Honestly, it's a ritual that should be outlawed in the ultra-religious Gilead. There's more paganism in what's going on here than any Christian/evangelical sect has a right to be appropriating. The pageantry is pathetic and you can see how desperate the wives are to have a child. But just when you might start feeling a little bit sorry for them, they pull out some bullshit like this:

"Would you like a cookie?" one of the wives asks June.

"You shouldn't spoil them. A cookie is bad for them," another wife remarks.

"Yes, please," June says, trying to remain serene.

"Oh, isn't she well behaved," the pro-cookie wife says.

"You can go," Serena commands.

"Little whores all of them," the anti-cookie wife says.

What the serious fuck? The hypocrisy in Gilead makes me want to scream. These women are forcing the handmaids to have sex with their husbands, and in most cases have put them in a position that if the horndog commander wants a little extra on the side, the handmaids can't refuse for fear of their lives.

And by definition, these wives are "unwomen" because they can't bear children. Why are they in blue dresses having tea parties, instead of shoveling irradiated soil in the colonies? The infantilizing of the handmaids is ridiculous too. It hasn't been that long since all of the women in that kitchen could have been in a restaurant or a shopping mall together. The handmaid that is being spoiled with a cookie could have been her yoga instructor, or her barista, or even a colleague. The Gilead Kool-Aid, however, has made these women forget any of that ever happened and enabled them to treat "lesser women" with contempt.

June goes into the bathroom and spits out the cookie. I would have eaten it. It was a French Macaroon! These twats are stingy with the sugar. There's a war going on after all. But I know why she did it. They can force her to take the cookie, but they can't force her to eat it. Spitting it out is the only defiant act that she can do at the moment.

When the baby is finally on the way, the wives get behind Ofwarren (Janine) as the commander's wife screams and pretends that she just pushed a bowling ball out of her ass.

Whatever gets you to steal someone's baby and convince yourself that it's yours.

But because of all the birth defects that happen, it's a tense situation until Aunt Lydia declares that Janine had a fine and healthy girl.

They don't let her hold her.

I hate these bitches.

We flashback to June just after she had given birth to Hannah, when someone tries to steal her baby. It was a crime to steal a baby then. And yet, Gilead has stolen Janine's baby. The wives name her Angela, but Janine names her Charlotte.

Janine sings "Every Little Thing is Gonna Be All Right," by Bob Marley.

It's so not, though.

Not even remotely.

Later that night, June goes to the commander's study, either walking into her "bloody end" or as Ofglen put it, "Maybe he just wants a blow job."

Fred has all the power here, breaking his own rules to show her how much power he has. "In here, we may be able to bend the rules a bit."

He wants to play a game with her and, instead of it being a sexual perverted thing, just wants to play Scrabble. The question though is why doesn't he play with Serena Joy? If they're going to be keeping secrets in the library, why not with his wife?

June wonders if this is a trick. Women aren't allowed to read after all. So is he waiting for her to drop her guard and then…gotcha? The Eyes show up and take her away in a black van?

But after the game, Fred just holds her hand and says good night. It's a subtle display that he could have done so much more if he had wanted to.

"Don't You Forget About Me" by Tears for Fears plays as June is feeling pretty good about the situation. She survived. She let the commander win. She even managed to do a little espionage for Ofglen's resistance network.

But the next day, as she goes to tell Ofglen that she learned the commander is going to Washington DC, Ofglen has been replaced with another Ofglen.

Self-Care Suggestion:

This was one of the milder episodes, leading to a false sense of security. So much could have gone wrong, but didn't. You want to know what happened to Ofglen, don't you? One more episode couldn't hurt, right? (Spoiler Hint: It is going to hurt. The next episode is awful in terms of trauma.) If Gilead is getting to be too much for you, take a break and come back to it when you're feeling stronger. If you were like me and want to see something good, it's going to be a long ride. So take a bio break, refill the beverage. Maybe sneak a chocolate snack and huddle back down for episode three. If you have a loved one, pet, or stuffed animal to hug, I'd recommend keeping them close.

Chapter Three: Buckle up, Buttercups

Season One, Episode Three: Late

"We've learned to see the world in gasps."
~ Margaret Atwood, The Handmaid's Tale

Trigger Warnings: torture, homophobia, murder of a gay woman for being a gender traitor, genital mutilation, hanging.
Gut Punch Rating: 5

Buckle up, Buttercups. This is one hell of an episode.

But before we get into that, there's a flashback to how it was before Gilead. In just one day, armed men came into June's place of work and all the women are "let go." It's the law now. And to make matters worse, the Constitution was suspended after a series of terrorist threats toppled the government.

Moira says, "They needed to do it this way. All the jobs and all the banks at the same time. Otherwise could you imagine the airports?"

First, Gilead slaughtered the Senate

Then, they went under martial law.

Then, they suspended the Constitution.

Then, they made laws.

Freaking out yet? How close is this to real life?

First, they elect a President that wants to do shit like this.

Then, they control the Senate.

Martial law could be declared for a number of reasons. Coronavirus epidemic? Social isolation?

Then, the President suspends the Constitution.

Then, he makes Gilead-like laws.

It's not fucking fiction when you look at it like that. Oh, that will never happen, you might say. Yeah, that's what June and Moira thought. It started slowly. With small things being taken away. Small things that could be explained as only a temporary measure, each little thing building up to a big mountain of shit.

Flash back forward. Anyway, when June returns from visiting Janine and her baby, there is a surprise waiting for her. Nick warns her to just tell the truth and not to be brave. Everybody breaks. Not knowing if this is about being in the commander's study last night or playing Scrabble or what, she doesn't know what to expect. June prays to herself that they don't hurt her. She's afraid of the pain, of potentially losing a hand or an eye. She pleads to herself to allow them to rape her and to be good, she just doesn't want to feel pain.

Aunt Lydia gives her a zot with her cattle prod before the Eye starts with his questions about Ofglen. They punish June for being Ofglen's friend and not reporting that Ofglen was a gender traitor (gay).

June and Aunt Lydia have a scripture battle which ends in Aunt Lydia zapping her once again with a cattle prod. However, Serena saves her by declaring that June is pregnant—which is more wishful thinking than anything else at this point.

Aunt Lydia turns away in horror, considering what damage she could have done to the unborn child. Aunt Lydia is all about the children. I can't figure her out. One the one hand, she's a terrible abuser of these women. She brainwashes them. She acts like a drill sergeant… and then there are moments when I almost believe her kindness towards them. What the hell was Aunt Lydia's deal pre-Gilead that turned her into what we see here?

The scene changes to what's going on with Ofglen. She tries, but fails, to escape by seducing a guard, and she and her Martha lover are brought before the commanders and declared guilty. The Martha is sentenced to death by hanging and Ofglen is sentenced to "redemption"—whatever that means. But the only reason she isn't hanging alongside her lover is because her womb is fertile.

Later, when June is sitting in the dark, Nick sneaks into her room and gives her some ice for her bruises.

"I should have just driven away with you," Nick says, and suddenly I'm #teamNick. He's no Aidan Quinn, but I like him a lot better than the Aidan Quinn character.

It turns out June is not pregnant because her period has started.

Flash back to pre-Gilead America. Moira and June go to a demonstration in order to protest their rights being taken away as women. The protestors are confronted by men with shields and guns, who open fire into the crowd. "Heart of Glass" by Blondie plays while bombs go off and storefronts are shattered from bullets and the concussions.

Back in present day Gilead, June walks in on Serena rearranging for the nursery. Serena calls June her beautiful miracle, kissing her hand, but when Offred corrects her that she's not pregnant, Serena throws her to the floor, telling her she's not allowed to leave. Completely unhinged, Serena screams, "Do you understand me?" and threatens that "things could get much worse for you."

What the fuck is Serena's problem? I get that she wants a child because she's got nothing else to do with her life except knit and go to baby shower pantomimes, but she is one violent bitch. I hope before the season ends someone—preferably June—punches her right in the kisser.

Ofglen gets up from her hospital bed. She's wearing a diaper sort of thing around her pelvic area. Aunt Lydia comes in and calls her Emily, and in her sweet Aunt voice tells her that, "You won't want what you can't have."

Gilead has removed Emily's clitoris.

The end song, "Waiting for Something" by Jay Reatard is a jagged punk song that has a frenetic and manic energy, reeking with desperation and I'm feeling every little pulse and beat.

Self-Care Suggestion:

Take a break. Things are looking hopeless. Go outside for a walk, clear your head. Watch a comedy. Stay off social media. It will just ramp up any fear and paranoia you have lurking around from watching this episode. As far as we know, Moira is dead. Emily is outed as a member of the resistance and has been mutilated. June is in trouble for not being pregnant, and Janine has a serious case of the delusions. Give it a few days if you can. There's a lot to process here. When you're ready, episode four is a doozy too.

Chapter Four: This Shit is Contagious

Season One, Episode Four: Nolite Te Bastardes Carborundorum

"Don't let the bastards grind you down."
~ Margaret Atwood, The Handmaid's Tale

Trigger Warnings: Rape, torture, descent into madness
Gut Punch Rating: 3

"Daydream Believer" by the Monkees plays as June flashes back to a happier time with Hannah and Luke.

Banished to her room for 13 days so far, June starts to lose her grip on sanity. Like Moira said, this shit is contagious. As she lies down on the floor sobbing, she sees Latin words dug into the closet door. It's a message from the previous Offred to her: *Nolite Te Bastardes Carborundorum.*

Just like when Moira wrote "Aunt Lydia sux" on the bathroom wall in the Red Center, it centers her a little bit. She's not the only one going through this.

We see a little of what it was like pre-Gilead with Serena giving good advice to Fred, but after Gilead, he wants no part of it. An Aunt has escaped and given a tell-all interview to the Toronto Sun. Fred tells Serena not to worry her pretty little head over it, that they've got good men working on the problem. That must really burn Serena's ass something fierce. After all, Gilead was partly her idea. She must have thought she'd be one of the exceptions.

Surprise bitch. You fought for this. Now, you've got to live with it.

It's very apparent that Serena is intelligent, probably even more so than Fred. It would be a good idea to listen to what she has to say and treat her as a true partner, but that would go against everything that Gilead stands for. Have a nice big patriarch sandwich Serena.

June goes to the doctor for a checkup because the ceremony is tonight, and he offers to impregnate her. If she doesn't get pregnant, he says, they'll blame her and not the commander. When she refuses, because that's illegal, he tells her that everyone is doing it because most of the commanders are firing blanks.

Here's our first proof that the purity of Gilead is a lie. The commanders are just as corrupt as the world they claimed to have destroyed and rebuilt. Only, their corruption is done in secret, in power plays to keep the masses ignorant. It's very George Orwell's *Animal Farm* in that way.

As Nick drives her back to the Waterfords, we see that the combination of solitary confinement and the casual way men talk about impregnating her has broken June, and she starts screaming and crying and banging on the window.

June apologizes to Serena and begs to be let out, but Serena just sends her up to her room. Serena's going to be a *great* mother, if this is any example of how she's planning on punishing a child.

Next scene is a flashback to Moira escaping from The Red Center with Offred. After tricking an Aunt into the bathroom and ganging up on her, they strip her down and steal her brown clothes and identity. This is a great scene, but I'm yelling at the TV, "Tie her up better than that. Gag her better than that. You don't want them to find her for a long time."

Back in the present, Fred comes to the ceremony early to ask June for a Scrabble rematch. At the ceremony, he has a hard time—or a not hard time—getting it up. We get a small glimpse into the state of their marriage as Serene follows him out of the room, offering to give him a blow job, only to be turned down.

Offred realizes Fred needs to connect to her, that this isn't just procreation for him. It's ego. He doesn't want to rape June. He wants her to want him too.

Delusional much?

Flashback to the escape. I had always wondered in the movie why Kate didn't go with Moira. At least here, June tried. But she got caught, and the Aunt they tied up whipped the soles of her feet bloody as a punishment.

Then we're back in present-day Gilead in Waterford's study. Offred sees a way to manipulate Fred, using his need to connect with her. When he challenges one of her Scrabble words, she sees a Latin grammar book by the dictionary and decides to ask him the meaning of the phrase, *Nolite Te Bastardes Carborundorum.*

He shows her it was written to him by a buddy from school, pre-Gilead. It's a made-up Latin phrase that roughly translates to "Don't let the bastards grind you down." So much subtext is happening now.

Fred knows the only way June could possibly know that phrase is from the Offred before her. And June knows her hand is at risk if she admits that she read it. At the very least, she'll lose a finger.

Has the first Offred been in this study? Has she played Scrabble and the mental mind games Fred seems to crave? Did she say the wrong thing—do the wrong thing—and was killed for it?

Fred assumes that she knew the other Offred, though, tells her that she hung herself. "I suppose she found her life unbearable."

He supposes.

So is that what the Scrabble games are all about? To make June's life in between rapings more bearable?

June sees her chance to use this to her advantage. Mentioning that she's ready to give up, she appeals to Fred's benevolent sexism to get her out of house arrest in her bedroom—completely undermining Serena's limited (illusionary?) authority in the Waterford household.

The episode ends in the past where the Aunts drag a bleeding June to her cot and dumps her there. At night the handmaids funnel in, each of them dropping off a small amount of food. It's a dangerous act of defiance for them, but one of solidarity. They're all in the same boat and they admire that June and Moira tried to escape.

It was great to see Moira get on the train, but we know that in the present Janine said that she was dead. Dead as the handmaid that scribbled the Latin message into the wood of the closet.

Self-Care Suggestion:

Don't let the bastards grind you down either. Get up and take a walk. Get some fresh air. Do some stretches. Maybe play Words with Friends on your phone or a game of Scrabble in real life. Don't let anyone win.

Chapter Five: Hypocrite Thy Name is Gilead

Season One, Episode Four: Faithful

"Faith is only a word, embroidered."
~ *Margaret Atwood, The Handmaid's Tale*

Trigger Warnings: Rape, vehicular manslaughter
Gut Punch Rating: 1
Favorite Quote: "Every love story is a tragedy if you wait long enough." ~ Fred

"It's not allowed," June says.

"It is with me," Fred tells her.

Seems like a lot of things in Gilead are allowed, as long as it's kept on the down low.

As the episode opens up, June wonders why Serena calls her out into the garden. She assumes Serena found out about her nights of Scrabble, or reading fashion magazines, and briefly she considers killing Serena before the Eye's black van can come for her.

But then Serena suggests that she sleep with another man.

When June said it's forbidden, Serena says well yes, officially. But unofficially, it happens all the time. June said she heard rumors about doctors, but doctors tend to blackmail the commanders, apparently. Serena seems to know a lot about this and suggests Nick. June's only other choice if she doesn't get pregnant soon, is to go to the colonies, so she agrees to have Nick stick his dick in her and see if his swimmers work.

Apparently, all these rules are only rules if you get caught.

Anyway, no time like the present, so up they go to Nick's apartment where he's looking pretty uncomfortable. He drops trou

31

and goes at it like a dutiful guardian. June tries to catch his eye, but he can't bring himself to look at her. It's over relatively quickly and everyone seems relieved.

Serena "not watching" Nick try to impregnate June is creepy.

But Fred touching June during the ceremony later that evening is double creepy.

Is he trying to get her killed? Serena would lose her ever-loving shit if she saw that. Luckily, she was looking away and probably jonesing for a cigarette and a good book.

In the next scene, Emily is back from her "redemption" of having her clit cut off and watching her lover hung to death. Now she's Ofsteven and her replacement Ofglen wants no part of the resistance.

New Ofglen used to be a junkie and sold her body. Now she's clean and has people who are nice to her, so she doesn't want to do anything to mess this up. New Ofglen is determined that June is not going to get her in trouble.

Meanwhile, June is worried about cheating on her husband Luke and flashes back to when Luke was still married, but seeing her. Her adultery is something that she's going to stew upon for a few episodes. Part of her is wondering if this is her punishment for stealing Luke away from his wife.

Ofsteven/Emily has found a home with a compassionate wife, and while it's nice to see a little humanity—the wife offers to be sick this month—Emily remarks that she can't be sick every month.

Back in the commander's study, June is full of fire and tells him that it's too risky for him to touch her like a lover during the ceremony. But Fred is full of cynicism. Or bullshit.

Your choice.

"Love was never more than lust with a good marketing," he says, which is interesting considering he's supposed to be in love with Serena and yet won't have sex with her.

"Maybe for you, not for me," June retorts.

Fred tries to justify that Gilead was all about making the world better, but even he admits that, "Better never means better for everyone. It's always worse for some."

Later on that evening, Nick admits to being an Eye—one of the Gilead spies. He apologizes to June because he couldn't say no to Mrs. Waterford when she asked. There was some connection there,

32

and I think Nick believes he has probably blown any chance for a friendship with June.

While the handmaids are out, June find out that the Mayday resistance gets their name from a French phrase, M'aidez—Help Me. Emily is also there having "recovered" from her redemption and freshly raped by her "nice" commander, when she suddenly snaps. Emily steals a car and runs over a guard before they manage to stop and haul her away. The handmaids try not to cheer and June remarks that Emily looked invincible.

She goes up to Nick's little apartment on her own that night, without Mrs. Waterford watching, and with Nina Simone crooning, "I want a little sugar in my bowl." And together they have some consensual mattress-shaking sex.

Self-Care Suggestion:

Life goes on, even in Gilead. Take the time out to connect with someone through touch or telephone. Get a massage. Chat with a friend online. Have some consensual mattress-shaking sex of your own. Or just put on some Nina Simone and play it loud with your eyes closed.

Chapter Six: A Place of One's Own

Season One, Episode Six: A Woman's Place

"These things you did were like prayers;
you did them and you hoped they would save you.
And for the most part they did. Or something did;
you could tell by the fact that you were still alive."
~ Margaret Atwood, The Handmaid's Tale

Trigger Warnings: blood, suffering
Gut Punch Rating: 3

The handmaids have to clean the blood of the wall for the foreign diplomats coming that night. Can't let the outside world see the horror of Gilead; they need for the rest of the world to see them as a perfect Utopian society. Fred is fretting because if Gilead doesn't get a trade agreement within the next six months, their economy will fall off the cliff. And that means no one gets French macaroons at their creepy birthing parties anymore.

Serena warns June not to fuck up during the Mexican trade delegation that the Waterfords are hosting. June gets paraded out to meet the foreign diplomats and, surprise, the leader is a woman. Mrs. Castillo calls Serena out on writing a book and going to jail in the before times.

"I had a temper in those days," Serena said, in what could be the winner of understatement of the year.

Mrs. Castillo asks "the quiet half of the room" how they feel about Gilead, and Serena very piously tells her that God demands sacrifices, but that it's all worth it. Serena has had a lot of practice at putting on a calm and righteous façade, but her peaceful resting bitch face hides the need to put the beat down on this non-Gilead that dares to question her. The parent in me wonders what she is going to do when the precious child that she's been longing for all her life decides to assert his/her personality. Serena is an abuser, plain and simple.

Pushing a little further, Mrs. Castillo nails Serena down, asking her if she ever envisioned a world where women couldn't read her book. There's another telling pause before Serena comes clean and says, "No," but goes on to gloss over that with a bunch of "praised be" bullshit.

Mrs. Castillo also puts June on the spot and asks her if she's happy. There is a pregnant—no pun intended—pause and June whispers a lie to save herself from abuse tomorrow. She sidesteps the question and says, "I've found happiness."

Fred, of course, thinks she's talking about him.

We're treated to a Serena flashback and we see a different/younger version of Fred and Serena in happier times. We find out Serena visited colleges and spoke out at a rallies about domestic feminism.

And that she's no stranger to being called a Nazi cunt.

During the flashback date night at the movies, Fred gets a text message from his revolutionary brethren. They're planning three separate attacks in three weeks. Congress will get hit first, then the White House, then the courts.

Back in the present, in the office of infidelity, Fred rants until he thinks June isn't paying attention and decides to throw her out. But before he can, June decides to try her hand at manipulating him again and begs to stay.

Fred has her sit close to him and he touches her. He tells her to kiss him. She does. And he tells her to kiss him like she means it. So she does. But it lacks the passion she kisses Nick with. Fred calls her a sweet girl and tells her to get some sleep. Fred: 1, June: 0.

Back in her room, June brushes her teeth until they bleed.

The next day, Serena orders Aunt Lydia to line up the handmaids. Aunt Lydia isn't too happy about taking orders from a wife, but does as she's told. Serena walks up and down the line inspecting them like a drill sergeant, and tells Aunt Lydia to get rid of the damaged ones.

Aunt Lydia is a true believer, however, and tells Serena that the girls paid their dues and deserve to be there.

But Serena points out that you don't put the bruised apples at the top of the cart, a foreshadowing that the handmaids are the commodity in these trade delegation talks.

Janine doesn't think it's fair and Aunt Lydia agrees with her, but calms her down saying, "Sometimes we have to do what is best for everyone, not what is fair." Aunt Lydia promises her a tray of cake and desserts in return for Janine not causing a scene. Again with the infantilization of the handmaids. It's not the first time we've seen this. Janine swears she'll be good. "Hope to die," Janine promises in an eerie childlike cadence.

We see Serena in a flashback where she was not allowed to speak to the Gilead council because she was a woman. She was a part of Gilead from the beginning and has written herself out of it. She had it all. She had a voice. She was an author. She was smart and valued and loved by her husband. They were true partners. But now, in Gilead, she has none of those things. She accepts that and gives Fred her notes and walks away.

Back in present day Gilead, however, Serena risks a great deal by standing up in the middle of the trade summit dinner. Gilead is in shock, but it's her show business razzle dazzle that the righteousness needed to win over their guests. The handmaids watch as their children are paraded before them as other women's children, and June looks desperately for Hannah, but she's not there. She must be in another district. June makes a sarcastic comment that it looks like Gilead is going to get their oranges.

Alma, ever the voice of reason says, "Gilead wants to trade us, dummy. They want to trade the handmaids."

Later that night, Fred is pleased about how things worked out with Serena. "You're an amazing woman. I forgot." He forgot all right. If he would only treat her like he treats June in the study, imagine what they could accomplish? :shudder: It's a good thing for the handmaids that Fred has forgotten a lot about pre-Gilead life and likes the superiority his position has given him. In a flashback, we see Serena adjusting to her new identity of being a commander's wife. In addition to throwing away her material things for a closet full of blue dresses, she's throwing away her autonomy.

On the top of the pile of garbage is the book that she wrote: *A Woman's Place.*

Back in present day Gilead, June goes to Nick and vents. She's full of self-recriminations. Why didn't she tell the trade delegates the truth? Because they would have killed her and hung her on the wall, but she doesn't see that. She tells Nick her real name and they spend the night together.

The next morning June talks to the trade commissioner, Mrs. Castillo, and tells her that she lied to her. She tells her that Gilead is a brutal place. That they are prisoners. That they use cattle prods to make them behave. She tells them about the punishments, the gauging out of eyes, and cutting off of hands.

Mrs. Castillo is all, "I'm sorry, but my country is dying. They need children."

June begs her, "Don't be sorry, do something. My country (America) is dead."

But Mrs. Castillo isn't willing to help her. She gives her some Mexican chocolate instead and goes inside with Fred to talk to Serena. But Mrs. Castillo's aide, a man named Flores, tells June that Luke is alive. He doesn't know where Hannah is, but he said he'll try to get a message to Luke for her.

The fact that Luke is alive brings a whole new dimension to things. Instead of just sleeping with a hot guy (Nick) for the hell of it, now June has to ponder that she's an adulteress...again.

Self-Care Suggestion:

Homemade Mexican chocolate sounds pretty good right now, but I'm an old school "Eat your feelings" type of chick. I am a little excited that the rebels have allies outside of Gilead. If you can, go to a bookstore or a library and get a book to remind you that no matter how bad things are here, reading hasn't been outlawed. This episode was the one that I was finally able to go to bed after binge watching from the beginning. Because here was hope. If you're binge watching this too, it's okay to go to bed and get some sleep. Here's the hope that you were waiting for. America has powerful allies and Luke is alive.

Chapter Seven: Use the Force, Luke

Season One, Episode Seven: The Other Side

"You are a transitional generation, said Aunt Lydia. It is the hardest for you. We know the sacrifices you are being expected to make. It is hard when men revile you. For the ones who come after you, it will be easier. They will accept their duties with willing hearts. She did not say: Because they will have no memories, of any other way. She said: Because they won't want things they can't have."
~ *Margaret Atwood, The Handmaid's Tale*

Trigger Warnings: hanging, murder, blood
Gut Punch Rating: 3

Finally, we get to see what happened to Luke on that fateful day that Hannah and June were captured. We knew he got shot, but what we didn't know was that the Eye wanted to take him in for questioning. But as luck would have it, his ambulance wrecked on the icy road. After fixing himself up, he grabbed a gun and went back to the car to look for June and Hannah.

He's found by Zoe and a group of rebels, "an Army brat, two strays, a gay, and a nun" that almost shoot him because he was wearing the Gilead guard's uniform. They're going to take him with the other refugees they're helping. The only problem? They're going to Canada. Luke doesn't want to go. He wants to try and save his family. But he's only one wounded man and there's no way he can win, and they convince him that he will die if he doesn't go to Canada.

There are several flashbacks to pre-Gilead where we see what June, Hannah and Luke were dealing with as they fled their home. They were smuggled to different locations by various people who either did it out of the goodness or their hearts or looked away for a fat bribe.

For a while, they found a tentative peace in a hunting cabin owned by a man named Whitman, while they waited for him to come back with their visas to get the hell out of Gilead. One day, they're spotted by a hunter on the lake and they immediately pack to leave. The hunter comes back later, and Luke pulls a pistol on him, but it turns out that the hunter is one of the good guys. He tells them Whitman is dead, that they caught and hung him. The hunter tells them to take the backwoods because the patrols are looking for them.

The scene shifts back to Luke's solo escape. He gets to the border and Zoe shows him the people who fought back against Gilead. Their bodies are swinging from the rafters, left to rot in a church. The rescuers and their refugees barely manage to get away by boats. Zoe is shot and left behind.

Three years later, which puts us back in June's timeline, Luke is in Little America Toronto with one of the refugees Luke had fled with. Played by Erin Wray, she's a blond woman who no longer speaks because of trauma. She had been rescued from a handmaid's training center and Luke is trying to coax her back into the world of the living.

Luke has been summoned to the American consulate in Toronto to speak with the diplomat in charge. As he walks down the hall, we see pictures of all the missing people. And it's not just a few people. The walls are literally covered top to bottom with them. When he walks in to the office, the diplomat asks if he knows June Osborne.

You can see dread and hope warring on Luke's face. He confirms that she's his wife and is given the message June wrote to him.

"I love you. So much. Save Hannah."

I'm not crying. You're crying.

Luke laugh/cries and stares out the window. He knows she's alive after three years.

The song *"Nothing's Gonna Hurt You, Baby"* by Cigarettes After Sex plays after the credits.

Self-Care Suggestion:

Have a good cry, if you need too. Stock up on tissues and let it out. You are allowed to cry. It will make you feel better. It's cathartic. And as you cry, remember that the lost women are not forgotten, and there are people who are going to help get them out of Gilead.

Chapter Eight: Waterford Thy Name is Douche

Season One, Episode Eight: Jezebels

"I remember walking in art galleries, through the nineteenth century: the obsession they had then with harems. They were paintings about suspended animation; about waiting, about objects not in use. They were paintings about boredom. But maybe boredom is erotic, when women do it, for men."
~ Margaret Atwood, The Handmaid's Tale

Trigger Warnings: hanging, rape, manipulation
Gut Punch Rating: 5
Favorite Quote: "I will not be that girl in the box."

June decides to continue to have sex with Nick, both because she wants to and that the memory of Luke is fading. But who is Nick really? We get our first flashback into Nick's life. He can't hold down a job, reacts violently to criticism, and punches out his employment recruiter who tried to help him. But apparently that's a good thing. The man who later becomes Commander Pryce recruits him to join the Sons of Jacob and be one of the Eyes.

When June comes back to her room, Fred is there waiting for her. He wants her to do something different with him tonight. Treating her like his personal Barbie doll, Fred shaves her legs and holds up a mirror while she puts on makeup. Something is definitely up. He gives her a glittering dress and heels and leaves her to get dressed.

White Rabbit by Jefferson Airplane plays and I can't help but wonder where in Wonderland Fred is taking his handmaid, all dressed up in a costume that would get her stoned to death and hung on the wall.

He takes her to a gentlemen's club.

41

In Gilead.

What the actual fuck?

Nick isn't too thrilled about this. His jaw is clenched, and he's really pissed. It could be jealousy, but that doesn't ring true. There's something behind the dread we see on Nick's face.

Inside the whorehouse, Fred remarks that it's just like walking into the past. If the past consisted of streetwalkers with rich old white guys for pimps and customers.

It's a place where the rules don't apply, where any exotic combination of sex is allowed and celebrated. Of course, the prostitutes are the degenerates, not the good folk of Gilead who are just blowing off steam.

June marvels, "Who are all these people?"

And Fred says that they're high-ranking government officials, people from other countries that they're trying to impress. Pretty much anyone with power.

June shoots him a look and says, "I meant the women."

Yeah, Fred didn't even consider for a moment that the women were people. He tells her they like being here. It's better than the colonies after all. They're lawyers, professors, even psychologists, because some men would rather talk to an intelligent woman. Fred scoffs and rolls his eyes.

Then, across the bar, June sees Moira. She's alive. Janine had lied or been delusional. Moira signals for June to meet her in the bathroom.

There's a flashback to the last handmaid that hung herself after Jezebels. Rita is hysterical to find her hanging from the ceiling, and she and Nick mourn for the old handmaid. To them, she had still been a person. As the hearse pulls away, Serena just snarls at Fred, "What did you think was going to happen?"

Serena knows a lot more about what's going on in Gilead than a wife should. Again, I'm intrigued at her inside contacts.

But it explains why Nick was so concerned about bringing June to Jezebels. He's afraid that Fred is going to drive her to suicide by forcing her to be his own personal whore. It's not enough that Fred is raping her a few times a month, his ego needs for her to enjoy it. And he thinks that dressing her up, giving her fashion magazines and access to makeup is the way to her heart.

Because that worked so well with the last handmaid.

Back in Jezebels, Fred unloads his problems onto June. He says there are purges in other districts and that he feels there's a target on his back. It's all about him. As he tries to seduce her, June starts to cry. There's no way she can say no. She has to pretend to enjoy her rape. Afterwards, she sneaks away to the dorms to talk with Moira.

Moira tells her about the femaleroad, a play on words comparing the underground railroad to getting the fertile women out of Gilead. But Moira had gotten caught and was given a choice: the colonies or Jezebels. Not much of a choice for Moira.

Moira has lost all hope of escape. "Black van, feet first, that's the only way out," she tells June.

In Nick's flashback, we see Commander Pryce assigning Nick as Fred's driver because he's suspicious of Waterford.

"We're going to clean up Gilead, son," Commander Pryce said. And you know he's talking about shit like Jezebels. At least there's one non-hypocrite in the shit show that is Gilead.

Back in the present, after they get back from Jezebels, Nick is cold to June. He tells her "We can't do this anymore."

What? Fuck you, Nick.

June seems to agree with me. She says, "You know I didn't have a choice. I had to go with him."

But Nick doesn't say anything.

I had started to like Nick, but this judgey nonsense has me on fire with rage. He was supposed to be one of the good guys.

"Is this enough for you, this bullshit life?" June rages at him. "At least someone will care for me when I'm gone. Someone will remember me."

Nick sees he fucked up, but good. He says to her, "My name is Nick Blaine from Michigan."

"Under his eye, Guardian Blaine," June says. I love it when "under his eye" becomes synonymous with "fuck you."

To thank June for procreating with Nick so Serena can be a mother, Serena gives June her childhood music box. Swan Lake plays when the box is opened, and a ballerina dances.

June says, "It's a perfect gift. A girl in a box who only dances when someone opens the lid, when someone winds her up."

She writes, "You are not alone" in the closet next to the Latinese "Don't let the bastards grind you down."

And then June looks straight into the camera and says to us, "I will not be that girl in the box."

43

Self-Care Suggestion:
I'm still mad at Nick. Time to get some aggression out, which means cardio. Hit a punching bag. Run on a treadmill or up and down some stairs.

Chapter Nine: Praised Be, Bitch

Season One, Episode Nine: The Bridge

"I feel like the word shatter."
~ Margaret Atwood, The Handmaid's Tale

Trigger Warnings: Rape, suicide
Gut Punch Rating: 3
Favorite Quote: "Praised be, bitch."

The handmaids gather for Angela's baptism. Janine still thinks Warren, aka Commander Putnam, will come take her and the baby far away from Gilead. All those blow jobs have to be worth something, right? But Aunt Lydia delivers her to a new family instead. Janine is now Ofdaniel. And she freaks out when it's time for the ceremony because Warren had promised. He promised.

My heart hurts for poor broken Janine.

In the meantime, June wants to help Mayday, but Alma tells her that they need her to go back to Jezebels. June is not looking forward to that; there's suffering for the cause and then there's pretending to enjoy being raped by your smug ass rapist.

June's learning to manipulate Fred, though. She seductively comes into his office to say, "I just wanted the thank you, that's all." *For dressing me up like hooker Barbie and raping me in a nice hotel after a few drinks, instead of having your wife holding me down.*

Fred, of course, eats that shit up. And sooner than you can say, "Look at that, my dick is hard." He arranges to go to Jezebels that very night.

Even Nick is surprised by that and he's worried that Fred is going to get caught, resulting in the whole household getting executed. Fred is amused when June gets sassy with Nick and tells him that he just needs to chill.

Back in the house, Serena's knitting her baby's bassinet. Coming out to share a drink of kitchen sherry with Rita, Rita almost blows it by mentioning the commander is out, but Serena corrects her and tell her that he's in his office. Yeah, the office. Rita lost her son Matthew when he was 19 in the war, to which Serena's offer of condolences ring as hollow as Rita's "praised be" reply.

Back at Jezebels, June realizes halfway through that she's not faking it well enough. She's distracted because she needs to get to the bar tonight to get a package from Rachel.

But Fred shows that he's not as dumb as June thinks he is. He makes her have sex with him first, instead of having a drink at the bar. While he's not on to Mayday and the resistance, he thinks what June wants is a threesome with her friend Ruby (aka Moira).

June says between her teeth that they're not that type of friends.

He allows them to catch up while he rinses off in the bathroom.

June fights with Moira in whispers, telling her not to let them grind her down. She has to fight, because she pinky swore that they would find Hannah. That's the one thing that gets through to Moira. She is so defeated, like she has just accepted that she'll be at Jezebels until her pussy gives out, until it's death or the colonies. June begs her to get Mayday's package for her, but Moira refuses. It's too dangerous. They can't fight Gilead, and she leaves.

Broken hearted, June has failed her friend and the resistance.

In the next scene, Serena wakes June out of a dream about a family day at the beach with Hannah and Luke. There's an emergency. Janine is on the bridge with baby Charlotte/Angela and she's ready to jump. She's telling the world that she did weird sexy shit for Warren because he promised her that they would run off together. Mrs. Warren, of course, doesn't believe that—until no one else looks surprised at the revelation.

June tries everything to get Janine off the literal edge. "Change is coming. There's hope. All of this is going to be over one day, and it will all go back to normal. We're going to go out drinking. You and me."

And it works. Sort of. Janine hands the baby off to June and jumps.

Aunt Lydia cries "No!" while everyone else gathers around the baby.

Aunt Lydia fascinates me. She seems like she honestly loves and cares for "her girls," and yet will gouge out their eyes, beat them and

46

send them merrily off to be raped. She's evil, a villain, but somehow the hero of her own story. I wonder how she got that way.

"May the Lord keep you in his mercy, you stupid girl," Aunt Lydia says from Janine's hospital room.

Warren is taken away by the Eye.

Naomi lashes out at Serena who had been trying to comfort her, saying "We all know what happened with your last handmaid. Men don't change."

Serena storms into Fred's office.

June gets a special package from the butcher, who tells her to hide it until they contact her. It's a note from Moira: "Praised be, bitch! Here's your damned package."

The scene changes to Moira. Looks like she's doing her toilet shiv again. Covered in blood and disguised as a driver, we see her drive away. Go, Moira Go!

There's no escape from Gilead, though. Or is there?

Self-Care Suggestion:

It's hard to get rid of the feels. Each episode of *The Handmaid's Tale* sticks with you. Try writing a letter to one of the characters in a journal. It will feel good to tell Fred off or to report him to the Eye, so that he gets taken away like Warren did. Or write a letter to Janine. She could use some good thoughts right now. Or maybe to Aunt Lydia wondering just what the fuck is her deal?

Chapter Ten: Terror Tastes Like Gun Metal

Season One, Episode Ten: Night

"I keep on going with this sad and hungry and sordid, this limping and mutilated story, because after all I want you to hear it... By telling you anything at all I'm at least believing in you... Because I'm telling you this story I will your existence. I tell, therefore you are."
~ Margaret Atwood, The Handmaid's Tale

Trigger Warnings: torture, abandonment, graphic removal of a hand
Gut Punch Rating: 5
Favorite Quote: "Terror tastes like gun metal."

We're back in the Red Center, at the beginning. June is freshly off the cattle car and gets zapped with an electrical prod, being instructed on how to apologize. "I'm sorry, Aunt Lydia." Her voice is quaking and she is dragged into a dark room to be equipped with her ear cuff.

Ouch.

In a voice over, June talks about that look in all the handmaid's eyes: Terror.

Back in the present day, June hides the package, but as soon as she's ready to leave Serena is there cracking her across the face. June goes flying from the force of it and cracks her head open. Serena knows about Jezebels, about the slutty gold dress in Fred's office and throws it at June.

"Couldn't you leave me, something?" she laments.

Oh, fuck you, Serena. It's not like June wanted to be there or had a choice. What would have happened if June told Serena what was going on? It would have been June's fault for "seducing" the esteemed commander and she'd be swinging from the wall. And it's not like

49

Serena was concerned with who was fucking June. After all, she had passed her to Nick as long as it got what she wanted.

The Waterfords deserve each other, but I still don't understand why they're together when all they feel for each other is contempt.

Serena has lost her ever-loving mind at this point. She drags June into the toilet, who is still reeling from the cut on her forehead. Serena whips out a black market pregnancy test. Hmm, I wonder where she got that contraband? Does she have a connection at Jezebels?

After forcing June to take a pregnancy test, she finds out that she's pregnant.

"Praised be." It's like a switch has been thrown—from a screaming harpy to angelic mother in a split second because of that little blue line.

"You think I prayed for this?" June gasps out. "You think I prayed to bring a baby into this house?"

Something flickers in Serena's face and she spews another honeyed Biblical platitude, leaving with the pee stick.

Later, Serena waits in Fred's office with the Scrabble board out. He knows he's busted. Fred tries to overshadow what's about to come by telling Serena that they arrested three more Marthas who were planning an attack. Seems all is not well in Gilead.

Serena offers to play a game of Scrabble with him.

"You know the law," Fred said, disapprovingly.

"Yes, I do. I helped write it."

Zing!

But then again, she zinged herself. She wrote it such that she can't play Scrabble or read the Bible, and I think she's more pissed that Fred is breaking the rules.

"She's a smart girl. I imagine she's pretty good at this."

"We'll talk about this another time." I like it that Fred is trying to be man of the house and Gilead her out of his office. But Serena has no patience for his bullshit. She lets him have it.

"She left makeup on the collar of my cloak. Is that how you snuck her by the guide points?"

But then Fred goes all in and tells Serena, "You brought lust and temptation back into this house on your back and knees. If I sinned, you brought me to it."

Really, Fred? You and your wife had celebratory sex after the Mexican delegation and, because you both enjoyed the sex, you're going to blame her for your fucking of anything you want in Jezebels. Poor form. Boo.

"Everyone answers to God," Serena says, still zinging him with her pious bitchiness.

"And you answer to me. Go to your room."

Oh, he did not. But Serena is crazy. She's got this. She sets the hook out with this:

"She's pregnant."

"Praised be," Fred said, quietly and with a glimmer of pride.

"It's not yours," Serena oozes vindictiveness. And then goes on to twist the knife. "You can't father a child because you're not worthy. God would not let you pass on your genes."

BOOM!

Fred has drank the Gilead Kool-Aid and believes he's untouchable. But he underestimates the women in his life, June and Serena. Serena, however, is a true believer. I think she would have been happy in the Utopia that she believes Gilead to be, but it's all a fallacy.

Once the news is out that June is pregnant, Rita grabs June into a hug. She's truly happy about the child.

Nick is there like a ghost in the corner. He asks her about what happened, looking at the gash on her forehead. June tells him that Serena found out about Jezebels. And she tells him that she's pregnant.

Nick drops to his kneel at her feet.

June says, "Don't it's terrible."

Nick says, "No it's not."

Serena catches them and he gets back on his feet. Serena tells her to get her cloak, that they are leaving, but don't need a driver. Nick seems confused. Serena has access to a driver that obeys her and isn't Nick. Interesting. Serena tells June that they have a long drive ahead of them and not to touch the curtains.

Meanwhile, we flash back to Moira running across a snowy field. She hides in a barn and finds out by touching a dusty license plate that she's in Ontario. Moira has made it.

Back in Gilead, June watches Serena go into a house to talk with Hannah.

Hannah? As in the daughter that was wrenched from June's arms and that she hasn't seen in over three years?

Of course, June is locked in the car and can't go out and greet her daughter. But it's been three years since she's seen her, seen her baby. How could Serena be so cruel? I think it just comes naturally for that bitch. June screams her daughter's name and begs to be let out.

But when Serena comes back into the car, she turns to June and says, "As long as my baby is safe, so is yours."

This bitch needs to die. I want someone to bounce her head off a car dashboard a few times. What an evil thing to do. I hate Serena so much right now. I want bad things to happen to her. I want her sent to the colonies for being an unwoman. She can't have children, right? She needs to go dig some irradiated dirt.

Meanwhile, Commander Putnam loses a hand for his crime of lust with Janine. So that's something, at least. I think it's funny that Pryce told the rest of the commanders that his wife asked for the most severe punishment—because she was worried about his soul. You could almost see Fred's balls crawl up inside of him.

Later on that night, June comes into Fred's office and sits down. Fred must be considering locking the damn thing by now. First Serena, now his handmaid. Anyway, June asks for his help protecting her daughter from Serena.

"Is it mine?" he asks.

"Of course," she sweetly responds.

"You do that so well."

For the life of me, I'm not sure if he means that she lies so well or that she comforts him so well. It's possible it's both. I'd rather not give Fred the intelligence to know that the child isn't his, but I'm pretty sure he knows or at least suspects that he's shooting blanks.

Back in her room, June opens the Mayday package and finds letters. She reads them and is humbled by all the stories, but at the same time you can tell she's wondering what good will all these letters do?

Moira gets processed in Ontario as a refugee. She's out of Gilead. She's safe. And she looks like a deer in headlights. I feel so badly for Moira. She can't believe it's real, afraid that this is all a dream and that she'll wake up back in Jezebels.

Back in Gilead, there are three bells—a death knell. There will be a salvaging today. Meaning someone is going to die at the hands of the handmaids. It turns out it's Janine because she endangered a child. Why did they go to the trouble of fishing her out of the water, if they were going to kill her anyway?

Because every rebellion has to be punished and reinforced. Only this time it backfires. The handmaids don't want to kill one of their own, certainly not poor, crazy, Janine.

"Not too hard," Janine says, wincing in preparation for the stoning.

New Ofglen, the one who likes being a handmaid because it's better than being a junkie, surprisingly is the first to speak up, getting cracked in the head with a rifle for it.

June is next. She holds out the rock and drops it. "I'm sorry, Aunt Lydia," she says sweetly.

All the other handmaids follow her lead, doing the same, causing Aunt Lydia to lose her ever loving shit and vows that there will be repercussions.

Feeling Good by Nina Simone plays as the handmaids walk away.

The scene switches back to Canada where a shell-shocked Moira walks down a corridor to leave the embassy. And at the end of the corridor is Luke. She asks him why he's there and he tells her that she's on his list. What list? Family. Moira hugs him, breaking down into sobs. She's finally home safe.

June, on the other hand, knows there will be repercussions for not killing Janine.

Nick comes for her. "Just go with them. Trust me," he whispers.

She does. She hugs Rita and tells her to look behind the tub, where Rita finds the letters.

The Eye ignores Serena when they come for June. They ignore Fred asking them for their authorization. This is above even the Waterfords. Serena screams, "After all that we've done for you!" as June is put into the black van.

Yeah, all the rapes and the threats and the beatings.

June faces the camera and says, "Whether this is my end or a new beginning, I have no way of knowing. I have given myself over into the hands of strangers. I have no choice. It can't be helped. And so I step up into the darkness within. Or else the light."

American Girl by Tom Petty plays as the credits roll.

End of Season One.

This was how the book ended.

When I first watched Season One, they hadn't planned on there being another season. How could they? The entire book was that one season, and after watching it, I felt I had run a marathon. And I was still pissed.

What the fuck happens to June and Hannah?

I trust Nick. I don't think she's going to her death. But even if Nick smuggles her and her baby to Canada, Hannah is still in Gilead and only Serena knows the connection. That is not a happy ending. June and Luke still lose their child.

But then, they announced Season Two and said that Margaret Atwood would consult on the second season. Finally, I thought, after 34 years I would get some answers. I just had to wait for the second season.

"It's their own fault.
They should've never given us uniforms
if they didn't want us to be an army."
~June

Self-Care Suggestion:

Binge watch something else to cleanse the palette. We all need to get away from Gilead for a while, especially when the political climate seems to be leaning in a slide towards that fictional government coup. I had to wait 10 months to find out what happened to June. You can wait a week or so to remind yourself that we're not in Gilead yet. If you made it this far, you deserve a binge watching badge. This was a tough season. The next two seasons don't quite reach the horror and gut punches of the first season for me. I think it's because June slowly starts to get some agency and cracks are beginning to show in Gilead's foundation.

Season One Reflections

Music supervisor, Michael Perlmutter had some great musicals picks for Season One. If I was going to do a playlist featuring what I felt best represented the themes and moods of the episodes, it would be the split between two very different styles of music.

The first playlist is nostalgic, evoking a time in the not so distant past. These familiar songs being in the background while Gilead has its way with June brings home that this isn't some other planet. This is an alternate history of the United States. We'll see in future seasons how June's experience with music brings home her situation to her. From Season Two's "Hungry Heart" by Bruce Springsteen to Belinda Carlyle's "Heaven is a Place on Earth,", hearing these songs in the context of Gilead makes it seem more real. Most of the songs on this playlist I can sing by heart and they remind me of happier times.

I roller-skated to Blondie. I raised my fist in solidarity at the end of the movie *The Breakfast Club* when Simple Minds played over the credits. I got slowly drunk on red wine, chilling to Bob Marley. None of those activities are allowed in Gilead. In fact, non-secular music is forbidden in Gilead.

Lesley Gore's "You Don't Owen Me"
Blondie's "Heart of Glass"
Bob Marley and the Wailers' "Three Little Birds"
Simple Minds' "Don't You Forget About Me"
The Monkees' "Daydream Believer"
Kylie Minogue's "Can't Get You Out of My Head"
Nina Simone's "I Want a Little Sugar in My Bowl"
James Taylor's "Sweet Baby James"
Jefferson Airplane's "White Rabbit"
Tom Petty and The Heartbreakers' "American Girl"

But there were other songs this season that wouldn't fit on the nostalgic playlist. They are more modern, with angry and seductive beats. Angsty with passion, rage, and despair, these songs are so out of place with the vanilla placidity of Gilead that it is jarring. In the second playlist, there is a fine line of madness that June is walking between the wholesome "Daydream Believer" and "Fuck the Pain Away."

Peaches' "Fuck the Pain Away"
Jay Reatard's "Waiting for Something"
Daft Beatles, Blondie, and Philip Glass (Crabtree Remix) "Heart of Glass"
Cigarettes After Sex's "Nothing's Gonna Hurt You Baby"
Wildfire (featuring Little Dragon)'s "SBTRKT"
Johann Johannson's "Faithful"
ODESZA's "Bloom"
The Knife's "Wrap Your Arms Around Me"

The orchestral score is equally haunting and unforgettable. It's almost a character, a Greek chorus, filling in the places left raw by the narrative. Composer Adam Taylor, the BYI Women's Chorus, Penguin Café Orchestra, and cellist Hildur Guonadottir all weave their magic to underline the tension and heartbreak. You can get Adam Taylor's soundtrack through Lakeshore Records. The album *The Handmaid's Tale—Original HULU Series Soundtrack* features his score for Season One.

SEASON TWO

Chapter Eleven: Take Me Out to the Ballgame

Season Two, Episode One: June

"Our father who art in heaven. Seriously?
What the actual fuck?" ~June

Trigger Warnings: torture, blood
Gut Punch Rating: 5

Season Two takes up immediately from where we left off and I'm so excited. We're finally off book. Anything can happen and what comes next is canon. What really happens to June? Is she going to that mountain nirvana from the movie? Or is she going somewhere more sinister?

This season has me pumped for answers to questions I've had since I was 16 years-old!.

The black vans open up and all the handmaids are gagged and rounded up. Is this Aunt Lydia's consequences?

The silence is deafening. Harsh breathes, panicked animal noises and guardians pushing the handmaids forward. Alma shoulders her way to the front to grab June's hand in comfort, but the guardians force them apart. They are loaded cattle car style into Fenway Park, only baseball hasn't been played there in years.

What is wrong with baseball, for Pete's sake? Is it that it's the "All American" game? What could be more wholesome than baseball? Gilead is fucked up even in the details.

A scaffold looms ominously, strung with ropes. All the handmaids are put up on the platform, nooses stuffed over their heads and tightened around their necks.

"This Woman's Work" by Kate Bush plays as the hangman

59

prepares to hang them. The terror is palpable. One handmaid wets herself. Others clench hands. There is no doubt in their minds, that they are going to die. But as the platform drops, the nooses don't take. And Aunt Lydia comes in with a megaphone. "Let this be a lesson to you."

Mindfuck Aunt Lydia 1. Defiant Handmaids 0.

The next scene is another pre-Gilead flashback, where we see the small things start rolling down the hill. Little things like Luke having to sign off on June's birth control prescription. They talk about her maybe not picking up the pills. And what a major warning sign for things to come, gets pushed under the rug because they're considering having another baby.

Back in Gilead, the handmaids' punishment for their defiance goes on. Aunt Lydia makes them hold rocks in their outstretched hands while kneeling in the pouring rain, and of course, anyone who wavers gets electrocuted with a cattle prod.

One of the aunts comes out to whisper in Aunt Lydia's ear.

"Offred has been keeping a secret. She has been filled with his divine light."

You know Serena and Fred are behind this. So June gets taken inside to be put in clean, dry clothes, while Aunt Lydia goes off the deep end in her own way. Breathing heavily and crying, she goes up the stairs to pull on a church bell while sobbing and laughing.

Okay. We know that the whole handmaid thing was brought about because most of the population is sterile due to chemical or nuclear warfare. We know that babies are precious and that countries are dying out because new babies aren't being born. Certainly Serena has lost her God-damned mind trying to have a baby, and even Rita is more excited than June is about having one.

But Aunt Lydia sees babies all the time. It's her job. Her calling. Her place in Gilead's fucked up society. Her reaction is off putting to say the least. For such a vicious woman actively engaging in sadistic punishment of the handmaids, her soft spot is babies and it makes me wonder why.

When Aunt Lydia comes back, she and June have it out. Aunt Lydia brings her soup, but June claims not to be hungry. So Aunt Lydia decides to serve up a portion of guilt instead. She tells June that Janine could have gone to God quickly, surrounded by her friends, but because of June, Janine has been sentenced to the colonies where she will have a slow, painful death.

But that's not all.

Aunt Lydia tells June that her friends will serve their punishment while she is protected.

June tries to regain some power over Aunt Lydia by refusing to eat, but this isn't Aunt Lydia's first rodeo. She brings June into a room where another pregnant handmaid, Ofwyatt, has been chained to her bed for nine months after drinking drain cleaner. And she'll stay there until she delivers her baby, and promptly executed.

"Shall we get you something to eat?" Aunt Lydia asks.

"Yes, Aunt Lydia," June whispers, rocked to her core.

"Wonderful."

While June eats, Aunt Lydia lines up the soaking wet handmaids and brings them into the kitchen to burn their hands on the stove. Ofrobert—Alma—is the first. June sips her soup while Alma begs for mercy and screams in agony.

In another pre-Gilead flashback, June is given a hard time at the hospital because she sent Hannah to school with a slight fever. The nurse's assistant is vaguely threatening, calling her Mrs. Bankole (Luke's last name) instead of her actual name June Osborne.

This is how Gilead started.

Slowly, with seemingly minor insults and infractions, like when the new coffee shop owner called Moira and June sluts. Or when June's credit card was cancelled and all her banking information became controlled by Luke.

Back in Gilead, June is finally back home at the Waterfords, when Serena comes to her bedside to threaten her.

"Don't get upset Serena," June says with vicious glee. "It's bad for the baby."

In the next scene, they're in the doctor's office, where the doctor confirms the pregnancy. Serena comes closer to June, who flinches expecting another blow to the head, but Serena merely kisses her forehead and says, "God bless."

They leave her to get dressed and the orderly says, "God speed, June."

June finds a key in her boot marked with a red square. Outside her room, she finds a similar trail of squares that she follows down dark corridors until she runs into a truck. The door closes after her and quickly takes off.

Is this Nick coming through for her? Could the answer to my 16 year-old self be... both? Nick gave her up to the guardians, but then rescued her? In any event, I can't wait to see what happens next.

"Going Back to Where I Belong," by Sugarpie Desanto plays as the credits role.

Self-Care Suggestion:

That was a brutal opening scene. Elisabeth Moss does a fantastic job with her facial expressions and the camera angles are set up to induce fear and trepidation. But it ended with her in a truck leaving Gilead. That's got to be cause for celebration. Pop open something bubbly and celebrate. I think we should always celebrate the little victories. It makes the failures much more bearable.

Chapter Twelve: Revenge is a Dish Served Cold

Season Two, Episode Two: Unwomen

"Every month you held a woman down while your husband raped her. Somethings cannot be forgiven. It'll take a few more hours." ~ Emily

Trigger Warnings: hanging, poisoning, blood, nails and teeth falling out from radiation sickness
Gut Punch Rating: 5

What the fuck is the difference between the blue-covered bitches that can't have children and the unwomen? I can't for the life of me figure out why the perverted commanders don't just send their old ass wives to the colonies and make the handmaids their wives instead. It's not like they care what the women think anyway. I guess it's some Gilead thing that I'm too much of a degenerate to understand.

Not that I'm condoning any of the Gilead shit, but their rules and "sort of rules" are so infuriating. It's very much a George Orwell *Animal Farm*, "Some animals are more equal than other animals" bullshit.

Anyway.

In a Mayday safehouse, Nick helps June get new clothes, and she pulls the handmaid ear cuff out of her ear. Covered in blood, but ready to go, except Nick can't stay with her. He puts her onto another truck and tells her that he'll see her soon.

June winds up in another safe house, which used to be the *Boston Globe*'s headquarters, and is told to lay low and stay quiet. At least there's electricity and water in there. As she walks among the cubicles, she sees an abandoned high heel pump. The second, she

63

finds later in a newspaper pressroom, where the guardians had lined up the employees against the wall and executed them. The cement wall is riddled with bullet holes and blood stained nooses hang from the wall. Nick arrives and June wants to make a run for the border, but he tells her that it's too dangerous.

She freaks out. She can't stay here. She's free.

What I love about Nick is he doesn't force her to stay. He knows that if she leaves now, she'll be caught and spend the rest of her life chained to a bed until she gives birth to their child. And then she'll be executed. But if he tries to keep her prisoner, he would be no better than Gilead. He gives her his keys and his gun.

She takes it.

But they stare at each other through the windshield.

June knows she won't make it to the border.

Frustrated, she begrudgingly decides to wait it out.

In a surprise flash-sideways, we get to see outside of Gilead. Emily, the original Ofglen whom we haven't seen since she ran over the guard last season, is stationed in the colonies. A bunch of grey clad, defeated women are busy digging up poisoned radioactive dirt, separating it from the good dirt. Does that even work? The aunts travel on horseback wearing gas masks and protective clothing, and wield cattle prods to make sure the unwomen are working non-stop.

Mrs. O'Conner, a high-ranking commander's wife and adulterer, arrives in the colonies and is told that she has to fill ten bags a day or she doesn't eat. In a surprise cameo, she's played by Marisa Tomei.

Emily befriends her, which is odd because everyone else is treating Mrs. O'Conner with contempt and hatred. The reason why she's here is that she committed a sin of the flesh, but the Commander was too busy with the handmaid he didn't notice.

"What happened to him?" Emily asked.

"He probably got promoted," Mrs. O'Conner quips.

Emily gives her alcohol to wash her hands with, because the water is poisonous, and outdated antibiotics to kill an ecoli sickness.

"Why are you helping me?" she asks.

"A Mistress was kind to me, once," Emily replies.

We know that really isn't the case.

In a flashback, we get to see Emily's life as a professor and a biologist where she defends a female graduate from a mansplaining student. But it's a meaningless victory when the student comes up to her afterwards and asks, "When does stuff like that stop happening?" The answer is never. And this was before Gilead.

Then her boss, Dan, tells her that she won't be teaching next year and tries to spin it like it will give her more time in a lab but Emily sees it for what it is. The new religious board members don't want her to teach because she's gay. And she gets so mad at him.

"They can't force us back into the closet."

Dan replies with, "I envied your generation. You've had it so easy. I thought ours was the last one to have to deal with this shit."

And in another scene, she sees the word "faggot" written on the sidewalk, and Dan has been hung out his window.

Emily bolts. She and her wife, Sylvia, go to Logan airport where they're told that their visas—that were good this morning—are no longer valid. They get passed around and are next informed that their marriage is invalid, because it's now forbidden by law. Since her wife Sylvia is a Canadian citizen, she's allowed to go, but since Emily carried their child Oliver, and is American, she's detained. Promising her wife that she'll only be a day or two behind her, Emily kisses her goodbye, and Sylvia leaves for Montreal with Oliver. Emily watches as they go up the escalator until she can no longer see them.

Back in the colonies, Mrs. O'Conner is vomiting and in pain. Looks like those antibiotics weren't really antibiotics. Don't fuck with the biologist.

"Pray with me, Emily," she begs as she writhes in agony.

"You should die alone," Emily replies, cold and emotionless.

The next morning, Mrs. O'Conner's dead body is found hanging on a cross for all to see, as an aunt promises consequences. Later on, we see Emily tending to her plants—at least something is growing in that wasteland. New unwomen are unloaded from a bus, including Janine. Emily recognizes her immediately and draws her into a hug. At least the two of them will have each other until the radiation sickness claims them.

Back in Gilead, June uses what she finds to build a shrine to the dead newspaper employees, and the episode ends with a very powerful camera shot of her kneeling with two nooses swinging over her shoulders.

Self-Care Suggestion:
June might be free, but Emily and Janine are destined to die in the colonies. So while June is watching *Friends* on a laptop and Emily is potentially growing poisons as well as herbal remedies in her garden, you can take a page from their book. Watch a comedy show to get the grimdark of this show out of your head. Have a cup of herbal tea or do something outside. If gardening is your thing and the time of the year is right for it, maybe plant some perennials to give future you a jolt of surprised delight. Failing that, a nice long shower or bath with clean, fresh and hot water never hurt anyone. Bonus points, if you use that expensive soap or perfume that you've saved for special occasions.

Chapter Thirteen: Blessed Be the Fruit Loops

Season Two, Episode Three: Baggage

*"Raised your daughter to be a feminist and she spends all
her time waiting to be rescued by a man."*
~ June, thinking about her mother

Trigger Warnings: execution
Gut Punch Rating: 4 (if you believe in happy endings) 3 (if you're
cynical)

June's jogging around the office, six months pregnant, and I'm in
awe. She's been at the *Boston Globe* Headquarters for two months
now, spending her days obsessing over the Sons of Jacob and the rise
of Gilead. She cuts out newspaper articles and posts them on the wall
like a police detective's murder board.

In between conjugal visits from Nick, June reflects back on her
mother, Dr. Holly Maddox. Holly had been a feminist activist who
got June involved at an early age. In a powerful scene, we see them
together at a Take Back the Night rally.

"They were writing down the names of their rapists and tossing
them in the fire. There were so many pieces of paper. It was like
snow," June recalls.

But as much as Holly was a force for women's rights, she wasn't
so supportive of her daughter. She had given June a hard time about
her job, about marrying Luke, and pretty much makes it plain that she
is a disappointment, because she doesn't see what a shit show the
country is downsliding into. Hindsight being a bitch, June now sees
that Holly knew what she was talking about.

During a flashback to the Red Center, Aunt Lydia is busy

67

lecturing her handmaids. "We poisoned our world and were surprised when it started dying." In a slideshow is a picture of Holly loading dirt on a truck. She's an unwoman.

"At least it will go fast in the colonies," Moira whispers later that night.

"Not for her. You know she'll fight like hell," June replies, knowing that by now her mother is either dead or dying without long to live.

During the past two months, June has gotten a taste of normal life again. She reads, watches a *Friends* dvd on a laptop, has an exercise program and even a lover that stops by when he can. And all while she maintains the candles burning in the shrine.

"You have to stop stealing Rita's real coffee. She'll kill you. No joke," she warns Nick.

"You didn't wake me up," he says, looking at her "murder board."

"If I wake you up, you leave," June says.

Back in Canada, Moira is jogging. Since gaining her freedom, she's been helping refugees, living with Luke and the mute traumatized girl from the rescue boat. She isn't given a name, but the actress' is Erin. Luke tries his best to get her to come out of her shell, to meet people or talk again, but while expressive, she hasn't made the step back into the world just yet.

That is, until Luke and Moira are sniping at each other over breakfast. Erin looks into her cereal bowl and simply says, "Blessed be the Fruit Loops."

"How long have you been holding on to that one?" Moira asks while Luke smiles on the couch.

"A while," Erin admits. Back in Gilead, a good thing never lasts and pretty soon the driver comes back for June. She's on to her next leg of the femaleroad. Dropped off at a sign warehouse, she is met by a man, Omar, who is going to take her to a safe house for the night, before continuing to an airstrip by Worchester. The plane will come the following day, as soon as it's dark. June asks him who are all these people willing to risk their lives to get the handmaids out of Gilead. Omar says they're either brave or stupid or both. And there's a lot of both, he admits.

Unfortunately, Omar gets a panicked text that the safe house has been compromised and he needs to get the hell out of there before he's caught. But before he can leave her there, June stands in front of his truck.

"No," she says. She knows she's as good as dead all alone out there.

Against his better judgment, Omar takes her home, where his wife and son are. They're the Econopeople, the workers, the lower echelon of Gilead society. June ponders that, "if she wasn't an adulteress, if she went to the right church, if she had played her cards right, if she knew they were supposed to be paying cards," she might have been an Econowife with Luke and Hannah. Omar's family does eerily reflects her own.

June plays firetrucks with their son Adam, while Omar tries to explain to his wife that it will all be all right.

"I don't how you'd give your baby up. I would die first," the wife says to June.

"Yeah, I used to think that too," June tells her.

Oh if that's not painful foreshadowing, I don't know what is. The family leaves early for church, warning her not to answer the door and keep hidden.

"Everybody here listens to everything," Omar said.

"They really do," little Adam agrees.

Apparently the only way to get ahead as an Econoperson is to rat out your neighbor.

Before he leaves, June asks Omar, "Which one are you? Brave or stupid?"

"I'm not brave," Omar says with a smile.

It doesn't take long for a nosy neighbor to knock on the door. June hides under the bed, discovering Omar's prayer rug and Quran. While June waits for the family to get back, she cleans up Adam's room and thinks about Hannah.

But Omar's family is three hours late.

June decides not to wait any longer. Getting dressed in the grey outfit of the Econowife, she walks right by all the guardians with guns. She gets on a train, not even knowing where she is going because all the signs have been removed. Surreptitiously looking at the map Omar gave her, June takes the train to the end of the line and walks out with the rest of the grey dressed masses. Once no one is watching, she ditches into the woods and runs towards where she thinks the airstrip is.

And suddenly she's lost, flashing back to the first time she ran and was caught.

There's a beautiful shot from above of June running through a cornfield to an abandoned airfield. The cinematography in this series is breathtaking. From the blood red coats of the handmaids against the snow background, to the sea of grey of the econopeople going about their business, the color use is evocative.

June hunkers down to wait for nightfall in the abandoned airfield, reflecting on a happy memory of her and her mother driving in a convertible playing "Hollaback Girl "by Gwen Stefani. They're free and not arguing. She wishes she could talk to her mother so she could tell her that she forgives her.

And June hopes that one day Hannah will forgive her.

Meanwhile, back in Canada, Moira has hooked up with a woman in the bathroom of a club, but can't accept pleasure in return. She tells her hook up that her name is Ruby. The ghost of Gilead is still haunting her and she's dealing with her trauma the best that she can.

Finally, the plane arrives and June almost gets shot approaching it. But after she introduces herself, she's allowed to cram into the cargo section. At the last minute, a driver comes up and is also reluctantly allowed on board. June thinks about Hannah as the plane begins to taxi down the runway.

Disaster.

The plane is shot down and grounded. The pilot gets a bullet in the head. The other passenger gets riddled with bullets and June is forcibly ripped out of the cargo area. So much for that escape attempt.

Self-Care Suggestion:

Call your mother or your daughter, if you have one. If you don't, call or reach out to someone you love. Tell them you appreciate and love them.

Chapter Fourteen: June vs. Offred

Season Two, Episode Four: Other Women

"I have done something wrong, something so huge I can't even see it, something that's drowning me. I am inadequate, and stupid, without worth. I might as well be dead. Please God, let Hannah forget me. Let me forget me."
– June

Trigger Warnings: Mindfuck by Aunt Lydia
Gut Punch Rating: 4

June's ear cuff that designates her as a Handmaid is stapled back onto her ear and she is chained to a bed. Aunt Lydia tells her that she will be chained in this room until she gives birth, and then promptly executed. But Offred has a choice.

Holding on to her defiance and the self-confidence that she found during the last three months on her own at the *Boston Globe* Headquarters, she is offered the chance to come back to the Waterford's household on a trial basis. But it's hard to remain strong with the power that Gilead holds over her.

Chained up in the room however, she's reduced to counting the flowers on her bedspread out of boredom. There are 71.

She returns to Waterford.

While thrilled to have a break in the tedium, she's still full of righteous fury. Aunt Lydia is in rare form as well, remarking what a lovely homecoming this is. The commander even welcomes June back, spinning a tale about how glad he is that she survived the terrorist kidnapping plot.

What the what?

June muses that kidnapping is a story everyone can live with. It shows off Gilead's reach and might.

But Serena is not ready to forgive. She follows June up the stairs and takes her by the throat. June just stares her down and says, "Serena, as long as my baby's safe, so is yours." For all her badassery, Serena's greatest weakness is wanting to be a mother. And she backs down, thrown off kilter.

June tries that shit with Aunt Lydia, but Aunt Lydia's made of sterner stuff. She treats June like a child, watching over her as she bathes, making sure she washes "down there." Really creepy stuff.

As soon as June is alone, Rita hands her back the letters and tells her that she doesn't know what it's been like in the 92 days that she was gone.

Aunt Lydia gives June a nasty, but healthy, green drink that June throws up. But Aunt Lydia is unruffled. Puke all you want. We'll make more.

Serena finally gets to have her baby shower and finds herself the center of attention, amidst all the sympathy about how she missed the first trimester because her baby had been kidnapped. But June is still getting in some sassy zings, remarking that she's felt the baby kick. Serena clutches the knitted booties so hard, it's a wonder she doesn't shred them in frustration. Aunt Lydia puts a warning hand on June's shoulder and asks if she wants to take a break. June chirps merrily that she's having a great time.

The commanders are having a get together all of their own as they shoot clay pigeons for the patriarchy. Warren Putnam is there, minus most of his arm. Pryce has his eye on all of them, but especially Commander Waterford.

Back at the baby shower from hell, Serena is sucking on a cancer stick like it will make all the bad things go away. And Aunt Lydia comes out to make it all better. Well, not really. First she tells her that God will forgive her for resenting June, but she's got to quit smoking for the baby.

"Everything now has to be for the good of the child."

Unfortunately June is shit out of luck too. In the market, Alma tells her that Ofglen got her tongue cut out for being the first to speak out against stoning Janine. That's not your fault, she tells her. Not that part. Mayday, however, has decided it's too risky to help handmaids. And if that wasn't enough, Aunt Lydia takes June out for a little walk by the wall.

June is having a really bad day.

But not as bad as Omar is. He's swinging on the wall.

"Who killed him? Whose fault was it? June did this," Aunt Lydia says solemnly, being a one-woman shame circle.

"No, Gilead did!" I'm shouting truth back at the computer. Much the same way that I was when the handmaids were chanting "Her fault" at Janine for being gang raped. No, if the boys kept their dicks in their pants, no rape would have occurred. "Their fault!"

I would have been tased to death.

"Such a selfish girl," Aunt Lydia continues. "You chose for them."

It's not selfish to want to go back to her husband. It's not selfish to want her baby that Gilead stole from her, back. It's not selfish for her to want her current child safe and not to be brought up in a place like Gilead. And Aunt Lydia is gaslighting June into believing that Offred is good and June is bad.

As June is processing brave, stupid Omar's death, Aunt Lydia follows up that his wife is now a handmaid and their little boy is with a Gilead couple.

"The boy will never see his mother again. June did this. June consorted with terrorists. Offred, however, is free of blame. Offred doesn't have to bear this guilt. June did this."

June, who is crushed that the family that had helped her has now been ripped apart like her own family was, sobs into Aunt Lydia's shoulder. Aunt Lydia soothes her and says that all she has to do to be forgiven is to ask the Waterfords to let her back into their home. So on her knees, June begs the Commander to stay. "Please let me try and be good."

I swear I saw Fred roll his eyes.

But it worked.

In several flashbacks in this episode, we see June falling in love with Luke, who is still married at the time. His wife, Annie, as you can imagine, doesn't handle it well. It wasn't a healthy relationship, but his wife does everything from stalk June to call her out as a whore. Luke stands by June, but there's a crushing scene when his ex-wife sees June and Hannah happy in a coffee shop. They share a look, and the ex-wife walks out. June knows that she was wrong, but at the time, it didn't faze her. Now with the stress of Gilead, she feels the ex-wife's pain as she never had.

A lot of Gilead's creation came from the patriarchy taking the reins during a chaotic period of government, but a lot of the atrocities came from women turning on each other. Aunt Lydia and Serena Joy are the two biggest culprits, but what about the econowives turning on each other or the handmaids encouraged to stone another handmaid? Those little events also add into Gilead's power. Of course the reason they participate in the stonings is so they aren't punished or killed, but the seeds of women stepping over other women are strong even in pre-Gilead. June realizes that she had her part in harming another woman because her feelings for Luke trumped her empathy for his wife.

Omar's wife's words, "I would rather die than give up my child" no doubt are haunting her as she is being trained by the Aunts in the Red Center. Or she has been killed or taken her own life. In either event, Adam will likely never see his mother again.

Serena, who is perilously close to losing her mind, hits Rita after June mentions she had to give half of the stuff they got away after Hannah's baby shower. Serena then laments to Fred that she can't take June anymore.

Fred soothes her, telling her, "You deserve this pregnancy. You're not going to let her take that away from you."

Serena finishes her cigarette in the nursery and sneaks into June's room to feel the baby kick. "Mama loves you," she croons as she cradles June's pregnant belly. After she leaves, June goes to sleep in the closet. Who could blame her? She sees that the words, "Nolite te bastardes carborundorum" and her own "You are not alone" have been painted over.

The guilt beats down heavily on June's head.

"My fault," she berates herself.

She failed to escape Gilead.

She was going to leave Hannah behind.

If she hadn't been an adulteress, maybe Gilead would have let her family be Econopeople.

Mayday has stopped helping Handmaids.

Alma got her hand burned.

Ofglen lost her tongue.

Omar was hung.

His wife is now a handmaid.

Their son has been torn from his parents and given to another Gilead couple.

"My fault."

You can almost hear June's mind snap.

She started this episode so defiant, but ends up cowed. Her eyes are blank as she passes by Nick, and her smile vacant as she turns to go to market.

Self-Care Suggestion:

Do something selfish—as in for yourself. Get a manicure/pedicure. Go to bed an hour earlier. Make a pot of herbal tea and listen to some reiki music. Take 10 minutes and meditate or stretch. Put on moisturizer. Read a happy, comfort book in your favorite chair with a lap blanket.

Chapter Fifteen: It's a Nice Day for a White Wedding

Season Two, Episode Five: Seeds

"She doesn't have anyone to look out for her." ~ Nick

"It appears that she does. The handmaid is not your concern." ~ Serena

Trigger Warnings: forced marriage, child brides, descending into madness
Gut Punch Rating: 3
Favorite Quote: "He couldn't hold you in the palm of his hand somewhere else? Like Bora Bora?"—Emily

I can't lie, I'd love to see Serena Joy in a cage match with Aunt Lydia. We know Serena's got a good right hook, but my money is on Aunt Lydia, even without the cattle prod. However, as Aunt Lydia is measuring and weighing June to make sure everything is on schedule, June has gone bye-bye. The lights are on, but no one is home.

In a very polite pissing match, Serena and Aunt Lydia compare dick size while discussing the mood in the house. Aunt Lydia not so subtly reminds Serena that the child needs to develop in a harmonious household and if Serena can't do that, she'll have to take the child away. That's a lot of power for an Aunt to have over a wife. And when Serena catches Aunt Lydia writing in a book, her well-coiffed eyebrows nearly shoot off the top of her head.

"It's a special dispensation for Aunts. It's more of a burden than anything."

I'm pretty sure Serena would gladly trade her cigarettes to be allowed to read and write again.

"Blessed Day," Serena says between her teeth as Aunt Lydia goes to leave.

77

"Blessed Day," Aunt Lydia says back in a sweet tone that has the same underlying meaning. *And the horse you rode in* on is silent, but acknowledged.

While all this is going on, June is bleeding heavily. Is she losing the baby? She doesn't seem to react at all to the blood in the tub or in her underwear.

Later that night, Nick catches her burning the letters Moira gave her from Jezebels. "I shouldn't have these," she says, following up with, "I'm not supposed to be out of my room at night."

Nick hides the letters, but is more worried about her mental state. He suggests to Serena that she take June to the doctor. Serena is not happy at the sudden concern and protectiveness that Nick feels over June and her baby. Nick doesn't know it yet, but his days are numbered.

Serena decides to take June for a walk instead, so the baby can get used to Serena's voice. While Serena makes an attempt to bond with June over petty gossip and tearing down the other commander's wives, June robotically responds with, "Yes, Mrs. Waterford/No, Mrs. Waterford."

In a quick flashback to the colonies, Janine is still quoting Aunt Lydia and Emily is putting her biology degree to good use, using plants to make medicine. Emily is trying to reach Janine by telling her the harsh truth: "We come here. We work. We die." And Janine is picking wildflowers secure in the belief that God loves her and is holding her in the palm of his hand.

We're treated to two weddings. One is in a prayvaganza, where the most valiant guardians are given brides in a mass wedding ceremony, while the other is between two dying women in the colonies, officiated by a female rabbi.

In Gilead, Nick is being rewarded for his service by being given a bride.

"Doesn't he look handsome?" Serena snipes.

June just stares brokenly.

When the veils came off, I gasped. They're children. The brides are barely teenagers.

For a moment, I think that June will snap out of it. But she stays in her cocoon.

In the colonies, carefree Janine blows on a dandelion, but when

78

she sees one of the women, Kit, fall over and can barely get up, she mutters, "I want to change my wish."

Emily loses a tooth. She can see the end coming for her too. Anger is all Emily has left and Janine's sunshine madness is getting on her last nerve. Fiona and Kit get married on Kit's deathbed. She's gone by morning, but it's a small slice of joy and hope. The group of unwomen have found that love still exists, even in that terrible place.

Unfortunately, Kit's death is the last straw for Emily and she explodes on Janine saying, "Gilead took your eye. They took my clit. Now we're cows being worked to death, and you're dressing up the slaughterhouse for them."

"Cows don't get married," Janine retorts. She may be crazier than a shithouse rat, but she's making a lot of sense.

It's Nick and Eden's wedding night now. Serena tries to help the girl by telling her that lust isn't a sin between husband and wife. "It can bring you closer together. It should, anyway." It's not always about you, Serena. Jeez.

Meanwhile, Nick and Fred are in his study having a drink. It's awkward with a lot of subtext going on. Fred congratulates him and Nick responds with, "By God's grace, I'll have a child of my own one day."

But when he drags himself off to his child bride, he finds June on the ground outside in the rain, covered in blood. He takes her in his arms and screams for help.

Kit died on her wedding night. Will June die on Nick's?

No. June wakes up in the hospital, back in her right mind. She's fine. The baby's fine. She goes under the covers to talk to her baby. "I'm gonna get us outta here. I promise you."

Self-Care Suggestion:

Celebrate Kit and Fiona's wedding. Dance to your favorite song. Toast them with a glass of seltzer or champagne. Have cake.

Chapter Sixteen: Breakfast at Tiffany's

Season Two, Episode Six: First Blood

"You tried to kill my wife. I said in mine heart, God shall judge the righteous and the wicked, for there is a time there for every purpose and for every work. Do you know what it was like to see my wife in pain, to pray to God to save her? [kills man's wife] Now you do." ~ Fred

Trigger Warnings: shooting, murder, child rape, bombing
Gut Punch Rating: 3
Favorite Quote: "What about Mrs. Blaine? What is her bedtime, anyway?" ~ June

Serena is a little kinder to June at first. She lets June see the baby on the ultrasound and, once they're home, insists that she stay in her sitting room. Serena feeds her soup and watches her sleep. It's become so obvious that this baby is everything to Serena, because without a baby she's nothing. Her friends are all having babies. All she has is her needles and balls of yarn.

Serena can no longer read the Bible or write books like *A Woman's Place*. Her husband thinks having married sex with each other is a sin because they're not procreating, preferring to bang handmaids and women who are forced to be whores. He no longer needs Serena's opinion or values her advice. Even after all Serena had done for Gilead, and all that she had sacrificed and helped build, Aunt Lydia outranks her and could take the baby away. June being hospitalized can't look good in that ledger that Aunt Lydia keeps.

Serena arranges to have the handmaids come over for the world's most awkward brunch where Serena tries to get them to relax and act like things are normal—instead of the wives helping their husbands rape them each month.

Maybe they all ate brunch at Magnolia's before the world turned upside down? The fact that Serena can bring that up, and honestly believe that everyone at the table is better off now than they were then, is the result of the brain washing that she's done to herself. She's a textbook definition of a sociopath.

She lacks empathy, because if she allowed herself to think about what she knows Fred does at Jezebels, she would have to admit that the God-fearing/abiding/domestic feminism utopia that she dreamed about is nowhere near what she is living.

In flashbacks we see Serena being booed off campuses for wanting to speak about her book. She's called a Nazi cunt and a fascist bitch by the college kids, who obviously have her pegged. She wants the women to embrace their biological destiny because, "The future and the future of mankind depends on what we do today!"

Serena evokes a full on riot and her security has to hustle them out of the auditorium. Fred, in a great bit of irony, yells that Serena has a right to speak to them. "This is America!" he shouts. Meanwhile, he's planning to overthrow America and replace it with a government that let's old white guys have all the power. But yanno, by all means, let the Nazi cunt speak.

Anyway, as they're about to get into the car, they get fired upon. One woman standing behind Serena dies, and Serena gets gut shot. In the hospital, it's obvious that her wound has made it impossible for her to have children. When Fred shows emotion and sincere regret, she tells Fred to be a man. And what Fred takes that to mean is that he should hunt down her shooter.

And he does, killing the man's wife in front of him before killing the shooter. In video game terms, Serena hardened Fred and basically created the monster that is Commander Waterford. Or at least gave the monster a doorway to enter this world.

Back in Gilead, Serena's goodwill evaporates when June asks to see Hannah. But June's not above pressing her luck, and she cozies up to Fred while he's eating dinner alone in the kitchen. They're building a new Rachel and Leah Center (red center) in order to process even more handmaids. (I wonder where they're getting them from?) Apparently Fred's under a lot of stress because it's his ass if it's not ready in time to show off to the foreign dignitaries. June sympathizes and smiles at him, but leaves him to his dinner. Still, she's reconnected with him and you can almost see the wheels turning in Fred's narcissistic little brain.

The next day, Eden wonders if Nick is a gender traitor because he won't consummate their marriage. June goes right to Nick and tells him he better do the deed, because Eden is going to cause trouble. His child wife will report him to the guardians as sure as Omar's neighbors narced on him. June breaks down and says she can't lose him, but Nick balks at the idea of screwing a 15 year-old.

And June says, "Aw, you have to fuck someone you don't want to?" How tragic.

He does the deed with Eden and it's a cringe worthy scene. Eden thinks that this is her duty and what a good wife should do. Her parents have brainwashed her. Nick is obviously not okay with this, but it's either commit statutory rape or swing on the wall.

While that is going on, Fred visits June in her room to cop a feel and steal a kiss. He gives her a picture of Hannah in exchange for fondling her pregnant boobies. It's clear the payment for that Polaroid is sex. June stops him from raping her by claiming it'll hurt the baby.

The next day, Nick begs to be reassigned and asks Commander Pryce to protect the handmaid. Pryce gives his word.

Serena decides to teach Eden how to be a wife by making pregnant June pick up her knitting needles. June picks them up, but when Serena encourages Eden to try it, June rubs her pregnant stomach and says she has to lie down. Again, Serena is trying to find power by tearing a woman down, and this woman is already as down as you can get. June's about to give birth to a baby that she has to give to her rapists in an unstable home. Even if June was drinking the Gilead Kool-Aid, Fred is not a righteous man. And Serena is a violent, crazy hypocrite clinging on to her delusions of a perfect world.

The Rachel and Leah Center's opening ceremony is finally here and Fred is looking to show off the new center with an elaborate presentation. The handmaids are all lined up, ready to be inspected, when Ofglen—who had her tongue removed for speaking out against stoning Janine—breaks rank and starts coming down the aisle.

I've got to pause here for a moment. We haven't met Glen yet, but he has had the fiercest handmaids. First Emily and now this one. Maybe a baby isn't in the cards for Glen and his wife.

Anyway, Fred is annoyed. It's not time for them yet.

But then she pulls out a grenade.

Ofglen shows it to the handmaids who immediately break rank and run away. She then heads towards the stage and BLAMO! The entire first floor of the new center explodes in fire and shattered glass.

Ofglen was pro-Gilead. She had been a former drug addict and sex worker, so she liked what Gilead provided for her. Then, Aunt Lydia had her tongue cut out. And Mayday was able to get her on their side for the suicide bombing. The resistance had finally struck a blow.

Self-Care Suggestion:

Get bombed? I don't know about you, but I'm exhausted. This series has gotten pretty heavy. I think it's time for a couple of days break. It ended on a high note, with the resistance striking back. Maybe listen to the *Les Miserables* soundtrack or knit a baby blanket we can smother Serena with. Get away from Gilead for a while.

Chapter Seventeen: Offorfuckssake

Season Two, Episode Seven: After

"I wish I could give you a world without violence,
without pain. That's all I ever wanted.
And in your name, dear Lord, we remember them.
Ofryan. Ofleo. Ofhal. Ofzed. Ofbill. Ofduncan. Ofcharles..."
~ Aunt Lydia

Trigger Warnings: funeral, hangings, shootings
Gut Punch Rating: 1

The body count: 26 commanders, 31 handmaids, and a bunch of Marthas.

At the funeral with the black-cloaked handmaids, the dead handmaids are buried with their Gilead names. It's a stunning visual scene with the costumes against the white snow and the pristine coffins set out in the field.

In the van on the way back to their houses, June asks if anyone knew Ofglen's real name. No one did. Later, in the market, they tell each other their real names. They don't mind dying at this point. They mind dying being known only by their rapist's name.

Fred is in the hospital and Serena takes June there so that he can see their baby. Fred opens his eyes and smiles at June, before she hurries out to steal a few dangerous hugs in the hospital corners with Nick. They're both in shock at the latest turn of events.

Commander Pryce, head of the Eye and Nick's mentor, is dead. Looks like Nick is going nowhere. Commander Cushing is in charge now, and he's decided that might makes right. It isn't often I agree with Serena, but she says, "Guardians shooting Marthas in the street, and it's supposed to make us feel safer? It's asinine."

The good(?) news is we won't have to worry about another

85

Ofglen. Cushing has had Commander Glen Deed and his family executed for what his handmaid, whose real name is Lillie Fuller, did.

In Little America, Canada, Moira goes on a search of her own, looking for her fiancé Odette. She had been convinced that Odette had been "rounded up in one of the dyke purges. She was reclassified as an Unwoman, sent to the colonies." Now, Moira's wondering if that was true. Could she have escaped? Could Odette be looking for Moira, or worse be in Gilead? She spends hours pouring over pictures of dead bodies in an attempt to find any information about Odette's fate.

In a flashback, we see that Moira decided to be impregnated for a couple who was willing to pay a quarter of a million dollars for the baby. In order to pay off her college loans and get some money in the bank to start a business, Moira decided that was easy money. June was her birth partner through thick and thin, even as tensions rose. The ob/gyn that was handling Moira's pregnancy is named Odette, and after the pregnancy, they date and fall in love.

They were engaged to be married when Gilead exploded onto the scene.

"What if I don't find her?" Moira asks Luke.

"Welcome to my world," he replies.

Back in Gilead, Commander Cushing (who is a real tool, even by Gilead's standards) visits the Waterfords' home and catches June all alone. He tries to get her to confess that terrorists didn't take her unwillingly, encouraging her to roll over on Fred. While it has to be tempting, June is smart enough to stick with the devil you know, rather than the devil you don't. She gives him her simple wide-eyed innocent look and stands by her story that she was an unwilling participant.

Cushing leaves, vowing to be back.

When June relates this to Serena, Serena is furious. She knows what Cushing is up to and what a conniving little prick he is. After all, they used to be friends pre-Gilead. Apparently, he was a real "blowhard" when they all vacationed together in Antigua. But Serena knows how to handle him.

At last, she can be a part of what she helped create. Of course though, she has to do it under the cover of it all coming from her husband, who is barely conscious. With Nick's help, Serena starts drafting order after order, recruiting June to help.

Wait just a frickin' minute, Serena.

Why is it okay to break the rules when it suits you, and not when it's inconvenient for you to remember that you're not the only intelligent woman in the world?

June is up for the challenge and the insurrection that Serena is embracing. It could be a way to get on her good side—if Serena has one. At the very least, it's blackmail fodder to get her to let her see Hannah again.

Back in Canada, Moira and Luke listen in on a press conference covering the bomb at the Red Center. June isn't listed as one of the dead. He's comforted that she didn't die in the bombing, but he knows she's not okay.

Meanwhile, Moira finds Odette's death picture. She was shot and left for dead in the snow. It looks like she never made it to the colonies, leaving her fate a mystery. Was she one of the doctors who helped Gilead? Doubtful. Did she pretend to help Gilead while being a spy? It could be. Her name is read with the dead handmaids and I'm not sure why. It could be because she was finally identified, so she could be counted in the Gilead death toll, or it could have been something that tied her to the bombing. We don't know when she died, just that she died alone, in what looks like a lab coat.

In the end scene, Cushing comes back to the Waterford house, probably to throw his weight around and attempt to intimidate Cersei— I mean Serena—but is immediately arrested by the Eye for apostasy. Silly little man. Maybe he'll be swinging on the wall? Maybe he'll rot in prison or perhaps lose an arm. Serena sneers at him, looking iceberg chill in her blue dress as she authoritatively glares down her nose at him.

Checkmate bitch.

When Serena later asks June into Fred's study, you can be damned sure it's not for a rousing game of Scrabble or to read fashion magazines to each other. Serena offers June a chance to edit the proclamations that she's writing on behalf of an unconscious Fred.

June's click of the red pen is hauntingly similar to Lillie's click on the grenade.

Self-Care Suggestion:

See what happens when women work together instead of tearing each other down? Fuck the patriarchy. Do something nice for another woman today. Give her a compliment. Buy her a coffee. Send her a quick email. Mail a thank you note. Let's keep this going and build each other up.

Chapter Eighteen: Back in the Closet

Season Two, Episode Eight: Women's Work

"We do our work in the evening. She writes; I read. This is the new normal, and an offense to God. In another life, maybe we could have been colleagues, but in this one, we're heretics. I was already on the naughty list—an adulteress, a fallen woman as Aunt Lydia used to say. But this is new territory for Serena, I think. How does she feel about falling? She seems pretty fucking happy." — June

Trigger Warnings: Beating, baby in danger
Gut Punch Rating: 2
Favorite Quote: "I do truly detest knitting. To be frank." – Serena

All good things must come to an end. Fred is healed up enough to come home and Serena gives June back the music box, along with a white rose to say thanks for all the edits. It's more than Serena gets though. All she gets is a virtual pat on the head and ushered from the office she and June had been using to save Gilead. Don't let the door hit you where the good Lord split you!

Back at the market, Janine nearly tackles June to the ground. She and Emily are back from the colonies because the bomb made them short on handmaids.

"Praised be," a shocked June mumbles.

"May the Force be with you," Janine giggles back, remarking that it's such a blessing to be out of the colonies.

Emily mutters that the bomb is the real blessing, and everyone that helps Gilead deserves to die. Luckily, no one has seemed to

89

notice her outburst or Emily might have been put on the next bus back to the colonies.

June wonders if Emily would hate her for helping Serena and the commander, but then the baby ambulance goes by and Janine thinks it was for Baby Angela (Charlotte).

"We should just pray for whoever's baby it is." June says, hoping to avoid Janine losing her shit on her first day back.

But it turns out that Baby Angela isn't doing so good, and Janine wants to see her. June tells her that she knows it can't happen.

"You sound just like one of them," Janine accuses.

Serena goes to Fred and says if they want to save baby Angela, they need to bend the law because Gilead isn't exploring all of their options. There is a Martha who used to be the top neo-natalogist in the world.

How does Serena know these things?

"Who is he?" Fred asks.

Oh Fred, you ass. Again, not bothering to remember that a few short years ago there were women doctors.

Serena begs Fred to help, but he's all like nope, will of God and all that. He's still a little butt hurt that she made some damn good decisions without him. He's got to be feeling like his balls are in a vise at this point. His pretty new Red Center is slag, the resistance has struck a major blow, and he was made to look weak in front of the foreign dignitaries. Not to mention, while he was recovering in a hospital bed, one of his friends went power mad and tried to boot him out of power.

And the only reason why Cushing failed was because Serena stepped up.

Too bad Serena doesn't have a dick. Then it would be all right, I guess. Or maybe not. She'd probably be a gender traitor and off to the colonies.

June tries to get Janine in to see the baby, and surprisingly enough, Serena tries to convince Naomi and Warren Putnam to let her see Angela/Charlotte. Warren is on board with it. "What harm could it do?"

Aunt Lydia brings Janine in and gives June a hairy eyeball, scolding her for telling Janine about the baby.

"If this breaks her, I'll hold you personally responsible."

"Yes, Aunt Lydia, I will too."

For once, June is being sincere with her "yes Aunt Lydia."

So Serena goes and gets the Dr. Martha anyway, against her husband's orders.

How does Serena have this much power?

How can Serena be such a hypocrite?

Back in the house, Fred goes looking for June, probably for another boobie grab and a kiss to ease his butthurt, but she's not there. How dare she? He notices the white rose and the music box, and has to be wondering what the heck went on while he was gone.

At the hospital, Dr. Martha dons a lab coat, becoming Dr. Hodgson once again. The other doctor gushes about meeting her, until Serena tells them to get on with it. Gee, Serena, how many babies could Dr. Hodgson have saved if she hadn't been regulating to peeling potatoes in some asshat commander's kitchen?

After her examination, we see Dr. Hodgson telling the Putnams something they just don't like. Serena runs out of the hospital room to yell at Dr. Hodgson/Martha who is in the process of leaving the building.

It doesn't look good for poor baby Angela/Charlotte.

Janine starts to break down.

"Janine, would you like to kiss her goodbye?"

She nods.

In the hallway, Serena, being a complete hypocrite, screeches at the doctor, "How dare you give up?"

Fuck you. Serena. And fuck the Gilead horse you road in on.

"I am the best. Or I was. Unhook her from all those machines. Help her feel safe and warm. And pray," the doctor says.

The Putnams allow Janine to hold Angela/Charlotte while they fall asleep in the other room. Yanno, like concerned loving parents do.

Back home at the Waterford house, June and Serena say their goodnights, but Nick comes in to inform them that the commander wants to see them.

Uh oh.

Serena says, "Let me handle this."

June and Nick brush hands as they pass each other.

It turns out Serena had forged his signature to get the Martha doctor in to see the baby. "What's greater than saving a child?" Serena says with a trace of arrogance.

"Obeying your husband."

Hmmm, I thought the whole point of Gilead was procreation and bringing healthy children into the world by any means necessary. I guess raping fertile women trumps letting women be doctors. Fuck these assholes. I can't wait to see Fred on the wall.

"You've asked me to read over your work before," Serena points out. Not to mention, Fred wouldn't be in the position he is if it wasn't for her. His helpmate, his partner, his former confident.

"That was then," Fred says, turning to June. "Is this your handwriting?"

June confirms that she helped Serena.

Fred laments. "This isn't your fault. It's mine. It wasn't fair for me to burden you with such responsibility. I must make amends." I'm surprised he didn't rend his clothes in anguish.

"Amends?" Serena said.

He reads a bible passage that allows him to beat her.

Gilead men love to forgive their women. They love the opportunity to humiliate them and remind them of their submissiveness. June muses that "men are afraid that women will laugh at them, but women are afraid men will kill them."

My money is on Serena in a fight;. She's got a lot of righteous anger in her. But instead, she bends over a chair and Fred beats her hard, while June looks on. Fred makes her watch. I can't believe that Fred did it and Serena let him. I want to feel sorry for Serena, but I just can't. Not only did she ask to be treated like that with all of her propaganda, she demanded other women all be treated that way as well.

So, I'm glad she got her ass beat. And I'm happy to see her cry. But there's also a part of me that's trying to be a little sympathetic to her because she helped the baby. As June reaches out to comfort her, Serena puts her Lady Commander guise back on and orders June back to her room.

So much for the détente.

Up above the garage, Eden finds the pack of handmaids' letters that Nick rescued from June. Nick freaks out, telling her to never touch his things again. He's worried she read them, but she denies it. Nick isn't sure he can believe her. If she read them, he's toast, but then again, so is she. So he becomes as Gilead as the commander and storms out.

What are the odds that Eden was even taught to read? Women don't read in Gilead, but Nick knows those letters are a death sentence.

"I thought there were safe cracks to make this world bearable," June thinks. But there isn't, not in Gilead. She goes to the commander and apologizes, saying, "I was only trying to help you. I'm really sorry. Do you forgive me?" She doesn't do this because she's sincere, but because she needs to gain an ally.

He tells her to get to bed and get some rest for the sake of the baby.

Boy, is he butt hurt.

June meekly turns away, but smiles.

And then the miracle happens. Aunt Lydia wakes up to singing. At first I thought, oh man, Janine has gone off the deep end and is singing to a dead baby. Because really, that's what this show has brought us to expect. But instead, we see a healthy and happy baby, skin-to-skin with her mother cooing happily. Janine is sitting in her underwear by the window in the sun. The baby is miraculously cured.

See, Gilead? See what happens when you take a baby away from her mother? No matter how much Naomi wanted baby Angela, she couldn't love her as much as the baby's own mother.

"I only want to be with you," Janine sings to the baby.

Self-Care Suggestion:

Sing-a-long time. Sing Dusty Springfield with Janine or a song of your choice.

Chapter Nineteen: Aloha Treason and Coconuts

Season Two, Episode Nine: Smart Power

"Waterford, you fuckin' piece of shit!" ~Luke

"Commander Waterford, if you don't mind. And you are?"

"Luke Bankole, and you raped my wife!"

"You have a simplistic impression of my country, Mr. Bankole. We all know the media doesn't care much about the truth these days."

"Hey, hey! You're gonna remember my face 'cause I'm gonna remember yours, and this is all gonna be over someday."

"You should remember your scripture, Mr. Bankole. This kingdom shall endureth forever."

"Fuck you!"

Trigger Warnings: grief, rage, victimization
Gut Punch Rating: 1
Favorite Quote: "If you had done better research, you'd know I would never betray my country." ~Serena
"I thought you already did." ~ Mark

Up in her room June is considering the impossible, when Rita comes to tell her that they've been summoned. Isaac will be watching over the house while Fred and Serena go to Canada for a diplomatic mission.

Isaac is a pious little shit. If he's more than 19, I'll eat my hat.

Serena doesn't want to go because it's the third trimester, but Fred needs her to show the Canadians that women aren't oppressed and voiceless.

95

"Show them a strong Gilead wife."

I swear she's going to slug him. She must be fighting not to knock him on his sanctimonious ass.

Eden brings Nick real chocolate chip cookies. I feel bad for her. She's trying to be a good wife, at 15, and Nick can't treat her as one.

Serena comes to say goodbye to the baby and drops a bombshell. Once the baby is born, Serena is kicking June out. June tries to argue that the baby needs her, but Serena has had enough of June in their lives.

And just like that, any sympathy for that stone cold bitch has gone flying out the window.

In Canada, Moira points Waterford out to Luke on the television. At the embassy, she demands he be arrested. Waterford's a serial rapist and kidnapped Luke's wife, but the embassy's hands are tied. This is not their country. If the Canadians want to do business with Gilead, the American embassy can't interfere.

But they do encourage them to protest.

Serena looks out at the city, seeing women on the street like it was pre-Gilead, and her expression is almost wistful. Sure, there is graffiti and homeless, but she smiles at a couple kissing in public.

The Waterfords are greeted by a gay man and a woman. The Commander is quickly swept away into an important meeting, while the cultural aide gives Serena a schedule of activities with pictures on them—because the women of Gilead aren't allowed to read. People look at Serena with a mixture of pity and horror, and in some cases outright disgust and hatred.

While June and Janine are walking, Isaac tells them to be quiet. But Janine talks back to the guardian, who hits her and decides to drag June home. What a little shit. I hope Aunt Lydia gives him a stern talking to about that, because that's about all the punishment we can expect in Gilead.

Serena is definitely hated in Canada for her blue outfit. Winding up in a bar, a man walks up to her who she pegs as a reporter, but it turns out that he's a representative of the American government. The man, who introduces himself as Mark, offers her a cigarette and a new life.

The banter between Mark and Serena is electrifying. At the risk of shipping them together, they would make a great couple if she wasn't a narcistic sociopath. He's intelligent, and as fierce and determined as Fred used to be, only with honor and integrity. Yanno what? Maybe they're not good for each other after all.

"We can have you on a plane to Honolulu in an hour. You wouldn't have to go back to Gilead ever again," Mark says to her.

Take me! Take me!

"So far all you've offered me is treason and coconuts," she replies, eyeing his cigarette but refusing to take one.

He dangles the fertility bait in front of her. A baby of her own and freedom.

"I have a child on the way," Serena says, but you can see that the arrow has hit its mark.

"That's not your child," Mark reminds her.

"You don't know what you're talking about."

Oh, but he does Serena. He does. He leaves her the pack of cigarettes and his business card. Take him up on his offer.

Back in Gilead, Isaac orders June upstairs. "It's time for your nap." Seriously, if he didn't have a machine gun, both June and Rita would take turns kicking the shit out of him.

June asks Rita to be a godparent to her unborn child.

"I want my baby to know kindness. I need her to have someone kind in her life."

Rita promises to do what she can.

Back in Canada at the protest, Luke is up front and personal about June and Hannah. Fred sees it, but looks away.

"You raped my wife." Luke goes after him, but is held back. He should have lead with, "You stole my child." No one cares when a woman is raped. Not in Gilead and not in Canada.

Nick is taken aback at seeing June's husband.

In the hotel room, Serena is brooding. Considering Mark's offer?

"We made progress. Border security, extradition. You seem worried," Fred said. "Thinking about the husband?"

"No." Of course, she's not. When did she ever care who was hurt, as long as she got a baby out of it.

"It was unpleasant, but we soldier on," Fred says, also one not to worry about whose lives have been ripped apart.

Meanwhile, Nick tracks down Luke into a dive bar. He tells Luke that June's pregnant and gives him the letters from all the handmaids. At first Luke is belligerent, but then is grateful to Nick—which makes Nick uncomfortable as hell.

Back in Gilead, Aunt Lydia is measuring June and tells her that Isaac complained about her. June explains about Serena kicking her out of the house after the baby is born. If Rita is going to teach the baby kindness, Aunt Lydia is the only one powerful enough to protect the baby.

June tells Aunt Lydia that she wants what is best for the baby. "You know that this can be a difficult house and children need to be in a safe place."

"I know what children need." Aunt Lydia is not about to take any guff from a handmaid, especially not this one.

"In the time before, were you ever a godmother?"

"I'll make allowances, but insolence will not be tolerated." Aunt Lydia fires off a warning shot. I'm surprised June got this far. The time before is never mentioned, but before Aunt Lydia can rethink her benevolence, June continues to express concern for her unborn child.

"Any man who would hurt a woman would hurt a child."

"What are you saying?" Aunt Lydia isn't dumb. She knows what Waterford is like and his crazy wife.

"This baby needs protection."

"I would never ever allow anything to happen to a baby."

June smiles because she knows Aunt Lydia is the baddest bitch around and now the Waterfords on her radar now. They're walking on thin ice.

"I was godmother to my sister's child. He died when he was four days old. It wasn't my fault." Aunt Lydia drops that bomb right in the middle of the room.

There's more to that story, the core of Aunt Lydia, as to why the children mean so much to her.

Back around the kitchen table in Canada, Moira grouses at the letters. "I thought that package had C4 in it. Something that could make Gilead go boom."

"This could go boom," Erin, their roommate, said.

And the next morning, the Canadians kick the Waterfords out of their country. Luke and crew had uploaded the letters so that everybody could read what the handmaids were saying about the horrors of Gilead.

"We believe the women," the Canadian official says.

98

"I don't know how you live with yourself. It's sad what they've done to you," one of the women says to Serena as they're escorted out of the consulate.

As the Waterford's limo is driving to the airfield, the protestors are getting violent.

"My name is Moira, not Ruby. Asshole," Moira looks Fred dead in the eye and he is shook at seeing her outside of Jezebels.

The refugees sing "America the Beautiful" once the Waterfords are out of Canadian airspace.

At home, Serena tosses the Hawaiian matchbox into the fire, while Nick visits June and tells her that the letters from Jezebels got out and made a difference. She hugs him and thanks him.

"I met your husband. He called out the commander and scared him. He loves you. He told me he'd never stop. He wanted me to tell you that Moira got out too. She's staying with him now."

June cries and laughs. "Oh my God, they'll kill each other."

"I love you," Nick tells her, giving her a sweet kiss.

Moira is Hannah's godmother. She got out. It's impossible, but she did.

June talks to her unborn child, "I know I should accept the realty of you being born here. Make my peace. But fuck that."

Self-Care Suggestion:

I was really frustrated at this episode. I wanted Serena to defect. I wanted the Canadian government to toss the Waterfords in jail for war crimes. I wanted something more than having Fred and Serena kicked out on their asses. But I did like the power of the pen. The package that Moira, June and Nick risked their lives for, changed the Canadian's minds. It looks like Gilead will not be defeated just by moral outrage, but by economic sanctions. That takes a while, though, and I'm impatient. Do something that gives you instant gratification. Buy something that you've been wanting. Steal an hour to read a book or play a video game. Have a slice of cheesecake or a decadent treat.

Chapter Twenty: It Gets Worse— a Crescendo of Suffering

Season Two, Episode Ten: The Last Ceremony

"Did you try to find me?"~Hannah
"I did. I tried so hard. Daddy did too."~June
"Why didn't you try harder?"
"Baby, it's OK for you to be mad at me."
"I waited for you."
"I know, and I'm so sorry I couldn't be there for you and to protect you. I wanted to."
"It's OK. I have new parents now."

Trigger Warnings: Rape and more Rape. Just. Rape. And mother being separated from her child.
Gut Punch Rating: 11—Seriously. This is a grisly episode. You need to be prepared with a box of tissues.

I was warned about this episode before I watched it.
"The rape scene is pretty bad."
All the rape scenes are pretty bad, but maybe the producers decided to make it worse. Somehow. So when Emily was being raped in the opening scene, during the ceremony, I steadied myself and took deep breaths to get through it.
"You steal yourself. You pretend not to be present. You leave your body," Emily thinks to herself in the voice over.
This time, however, the Commander has a heart attack after he finishes, falling to the floor.

"Get help," the wife screams.

"Chances are better if I lay on my back afterwards," Emily says to her. She kicks him a few times after the wife runs for help, but he's already dead.

Well, that wasn't so bad. I mean it was, but it didn't live up to the hype I had heard.

Wait for it.

At the market, June goes into labor while Eden's husband leads gently up the stairs to the Waterford house.

Serena goes down on her knees and prays. "We did it, Offred. This is the will of God and we shall rejoice and be glad of it."

Aunt Lydia brings in the handmaids and here we go again with the pantomime. As Serena lies down on the floor to practice her breathing, a harpist begins to play and the other wives whisper encouragement. Serena looks joyful and happy. "You deserve this," the wives coo at her.

Back in Fred's study, the commanders smoke and drink and make ribald conversation about handmaids. Nick has to listen as one commander asks Fred if he could send June his way after the birth. Appropriate eyebrow wiggling and winking ensue.

Then, Aunt Lydia tells Serena it was a false alarm. False labor. "You might want to consider timing the contractions next time," Aunt Lydia says, with just enough exasperation to needle Serena into overdrive.

Serena is livid.

The fuel to the fire is June's pious, "I'm sorry Mrs. Waterford." It sounds like a big fat fuck you.

And Serena takes it that way.

The doctor said it was Braxton Hicks contractions and the baby isn't coming anytime soon. Serena wants to induce, but the doctor doesn't want to. Not just yet.

Aunt Lydia suggests vigorous walks, spicy tea and mango salad.

June knows she's going to another district after the baby's birth, so she visits Fred in his study that night to asks for help. "I've already lost a child. I'm about to lose another one. It would help if I could be moved to my daughter's district."

"I've been too lenient with you. Too indulgent. I've spoiled you. Get out."

I think Fred is butt hurt that she didn't ask to stay with him. He screams, "Get out" and seems to be suffering, but June tells him off.

"You don't know what it's like to have a child of your own flesh and blood. And you never will."

Then, she storms off.

Serena is angrily planting when Fred comes to confront her. "She's forgotten her place," Fred said. But Serena has lost her God-damned mind again. This time, instead of smacking June's head around, Serena decides that Fred should rape June to entice the baby to come out. And Fred, whose ego is still smarting, agrees.

It's a terrible, brutal scene and I want Serena and Fred to die in a fire. If you can fast forward through it, do. June screams while Serena and Fred almost kiss over her body, and it's total revenge on June for overstepping her place.

Later that night, Nick catches his wife smooching the guardian Isaac. Nick doesn't care, but Eden sees him and comes up into the house.

"Don't worry about it," Nick said.

"Don't you care? Why don't you care?" I feel so bad for his child bride. She's done everything she was told to do, and yet marriage and a home wasn't the dream that was promised.

"It's okay. You're not in trouble."

"I've never been kissed until tonight. I'm your wife. You just caught me cheating on you. You should care."

Eden sobs after realizing that Nick doesn't love her. Marriage is forever in Gilead and Eden has been brought up to believe that what she just did was a sin. She finally found romance, and a man to love her, but she's married to the wrong guardian.

Fred visits June the next day, all smiles, and sits on her bed. "I planned a surprise for you. I think you'll like it."

June is near broken, but gets into the car. Nick is driving. Fred tells him to be back in three hours before Serena notices that they're gone. He kisses June on the forehead, but she flinches. Fred tells her, "Don't let anyone see you."

Nick tries to talk to her, but June has gone bye-bye again. He takes her to a summer-ized mansion and in the living room is Hannah. June's daughter. She has 10 minutes. June tries to hug Hannah, but Hannah runs behind her Martha and hides.

Her name is Agnes now.

This is another gut-wrenching scene. It's agony, but don't fast forward through it. Grab a box of tissues because you're going to ugly cry.

As June talks to her to try and get her to remember, she finds out that Hannah's been punished and hit twice. Hannah finally notices that her mom is going to have a baby. She tells her, "You don't get to keep it."

That broke my heart. Hannah realizes that her mother won't get to keep her half-sister.

"We have to go right now," Hannah's guardian says.

Ten minutes wasn't enough. Hannah had just started to recognize her and remember her old life. June is forced to tell her goodbye.

"I'll always be your Mommy. Daddy and I will always love you. Enjoy your life. Love your parents. Be careful. Keep yourself safe." She asks the Martha to take care of her. "Protect her and love her for me."

"I promise."

"Am I ever going to see you again?" Hannah wails.

"I'm going to try."

The other guardian tells them to stay inside. June has to listen to Hannah call out for her.

"Mommy!"

June runs out in the snow for a last hug, telling her it's okay and to be brave. She loves her enough to know that this parting can't be as traumatic as the one where they were first separated. And yet, it still is.

The car races off leaving June crumpled in the snow, twisting in mental agony to match the physical agony from yesterday's rape.

But something is wrong.

Nick drags her into the house and tells her to hide just before a bunch of Eyes show up. They don't believe Nick's excuses as to why he was there. Nick is knocked out and taken away in the black van. The car they drove in with is confiscated.

June is left all alone in an abandoned house somewhere in the deep woods, in winter, in the middle of nowhere. And she's nine months pregnant.

Self-Care Suggestion:

Let the ugly cry run its course. Do what you have to do to feel normal again. This was a mother fucker of an episode. Hug someone you love. Hug your child. Hug everyone. Get an electric blanket if it's a chilly day and wrap yourself in it. Take a long bath. You'll get through this. Just an FYI, it doesn't get any better on the second or third watch. Listen to some happy music or watch a comedian show. Do all the things.

Take a break from the show. June's not going anywhere. We're not in Gilead. This isn't us. We will never let it be us. But just in case, make sure your passport is up-to-date.

"Stay in Gilead long enough, it eats you inside and out. It forces you to kill within yourself."~June

Chapter Twenty-One: I Went For A Drive and Never Went Back

Season Two, Episode Eleven: Holly

I'm sorry there is so much pain in this story. I'm sorry it's in fragments, like a body caught in crossfire, pulled apart by force, but there is nothing I can do to change it. I've tried to put some of the good things in as well." ~June

Trigger Warnings: Blood, giving birth without pain medication.
Gut Punch Rating: 3

June is reeling from the loss of Hannah and from Nick being taken away. As she starts to jog down the road, she realizes that she's not going to get very far nine months pregnant in the middle of winter. She spies a garage and tries to get inside, but it's locked.

Creeping out of nowhere, a black wolf growls at her. She heads for the house, keeping a wary eye on it, but as she's scouring the house looking for the keys, she realizes that this is Hannah's home. She sees a picture of her fishing with the commander's wife and sees artwork that Hannah has drawn. While she's looking around, June is struck with contractions as memories of leaving Hannah at day care assault her.

June realizes how much of her daughter's life she had missed while in Gilead and feels guilty for dropping her off at pre-school when America was still America. The comparison of Hannah crying when June left her for work, to Hannah crying for her as the Gilead people take her away, is gut wrenching.

June eventually finds the garage keys and the keys to what looks like a sweet, hot rod Mustang. Putting the key in the ignition, the engine roars to life. On the radio, she hears Radio Free America and Oprah Whitney's voice. It's the first real news June has experienced. There is life after Gilead. There are better places out there.

Bruce Springsteen's "Hungry Heart" plays on the radio while June closes her eyes and recalls what a normal life was like.

June gets lots of vigorous exercise moving up and down the stairs, packing for a trip the hell out of Gilead, and gets changed into something less conspicuous. She flashes back to when she was pregnant, but then the Waterfords show up.

June hides while Serena and Fred hysterically tear into the house and into each other.

"Commander MacKenzie," Fred yells. *Ah hah!* We now know the name of the family that has Hannah.

"Offred!" Serena primal screams.

Yeah, like she's going to answer to that.

Serena sees that June's red cloak and white hat have been discarded.

June sneaks around the top floor, keeping silent. She's finds a rifle.

"If you had shown that girl one ounce of kindness, she would never have left," Fred rails at Serena.

"You are such a fucking idiot," Serena shouts back. *You married him, sugar.*

"Fuck, when did you become such a fucking bitch?" *Uh wake up, Fred. There have been clues. Haven't you been paying attention?*

"They'll put us on the wall," Serena moans, falling apart. *Good. Serves you right. I hope you piss yourself before you die.*

"Yeah, maybe they'll hang us side by side, just my fucking luck." Fred is angry, but he's blaming the situation on Serena, when he's just as much to blame.

"I gave up everything for you and for the cause. I only wanted one thing in return. A baby," Serena sobs.

Jesus, Serena, there are easier ways of getting a baby than overthrowing a government and subjecting more than half of the population to terrible fates.

Meanwhile, June loads the shotgun and is prepared to fire on them.

"You've left me with nothing," Serena says. "I have nothing."

But June hesitates and the Waterfords move out of sight, leaving as quickly as they had come. I don't know if I could have stopped myself from pulling the trigger and killing both of them.

June gets into the Mustang, but can't open the garage door.

Bust through the door with the car, June!

But that muscle car does not have it in it to break through. June smokes the tires, revs the engine, and still that door is not moving. Fueled by rage, June tries to shovel her way out and falls into the snow to see that her water's broke. She knows that she's not going anywhere. The baby is on the way. And she's all alone.

Well, except for the black wolf.

June heads back into the house, builds a fire and gets ready to deliver her own baby. It's a lot different from Hannah's birth when she had Moira and Luke with her in the hospital bed, with Luke's playlist soothing her.

And yet, somehow, they're all there—even if it's only in June's thoughts and memories. Her mother Holly, who was late for Hannah's birth, smiles down at her daughter in a flashback.

June goes outside once again and fires the shotgun in the sky. "Here I am. Come and get me." After a lot of screaming and agony, the baby is born. Just as June names the baby Holly, after her mother, headlights flash through the window.

Gilead has arrived.

Self-Care Suggestion:

Go for a long drive. Play "The Boss" loud. I'm a big fan of *Born to Run* and *Thunder Road.*

Chapter Twenty-Two: Mommy Dearest

Season Two, Episode Twelve: Postpartum

"Love is patient, love is kind. It does not envy, it does not boast, it is not proud..." ~1 Corinthians 13

Trigger Warnings: murder by drowning, a sinister new commander, a father betraying his daughter
Gut Punch Rating: 3
Favorite Quote: "I'm wondering why such an important, brilliant man would take in such a shitty handmaid."—Emily

The opening scene makes me want to barf...

Serena is cradling baby Holly in a radiant sunbeam, but is still not fulfilled. It's been a few weeks for the Waterfords to find domestic bliss, and yet she can't feed the stolen baby they've re-named Nichole. Meanwhile, June has been banished to The Red Center with Aunt Lydia as her babysitter, only being allowed to pump milk and occasionally accept a bran muffin bribe.

I'm not sure how the Waterfords have skated away unscathed from this latest scandal. June's second escape attempt? They can't really deny she was all alone in another Commander's house to have her baby. Fred gives an offhand remark that Nick saved the day and that it was an overzealous guard who caused the misunderstanding.

Delusional? Table for one.

June's milk is drying up, and not even a quick meeting where she hears her daughter—but can't touch her per Serena's rules—can keep it flowing. June begs Commander Waterford to let her back into the house and surprisingly he relents, but she is confined to her room where she will only pump, not feed the baby.

Serena is just not getting the unconditional love/doing what's best for the baby thing that she should have learned from Naomi and Janine. She even tries to breastfeed the baby herself.

Delusional? Make that a table for two.

Switching over to another handmaid's tale, Emily is on a new assignment. She's brought to Commander Lawrence, who she's told is "an architect of Gilead's economy." And things are definitely different in this household. The wife doesn't meet them at the door, and the Martha is surly. Aunt Lydia is genuinely worried for Emily's safety.

Lawrence isn't like the other Commanders. His staff feels comfortable to speak out, somewhat disrespectfully, yet the Martha, Cora, has only one eye. It seems the Commander likes collecting damaged women. I wonder why he didn't request Janine then. Of course, Janine would probably spill everything to Aunt Lydia and get him in trouble for not being a typical Commander.

While he's sadistic, he's also not towing the Gilead line. He loves his head games. He catches Emily reading a graphic novel. He offers her alcohol. He lets her know he's familiar with every bit of her life—both before and during Gilead. Lawrence asks her questions like, "How did it feel to run over the guard?" Emily is terrified and tries to give the right answers, knowing she could lose a finger for reading or be up on the wall tomorrow for answering wrong. He doesn't seem to want a meek handmaid.

But when his wife comes into Emily's room that night and tells Emily that her husband is the monster who created the colonies, and has done many more evil things, I'm not sure Emily is going to survive this crazy house.

Emily asks Lawrence if his wife is all right and he says, "Yes. Life didn't turn out the way she wanted it to. She was an art professor. She wanted it to be beautiful."

Commander Lawrence is an enigma. He's got modern art on his walls, allows his Martha to talk back to him. He's kind and considerate to his wife Eleanor and he reads graphic novels in his spare time. The one that he caught Emily reading is *Maus* by Art Spiegelman. It's a retelling of Spiegelman's father's experiences in a concentration camp in World War Two.

I want to believe Lawrence is also going to be the architect of

Gilead's destruction. I desperately want to believe he has power to protect Emily. But hope is a funny thing in Gilead.

Back in the Waterford house, Nick and June share a tender moment, and later Eden asks June about love. June tells her that she should take love where she can find it, because it makes life bearable. Unfortunately, Eden is in love with Isaac and they go running off together.

Fred is livid—because it's all about him after all. It doesn't take any time at all to capture the young lovers and they're brought to the local pool. Nick begs Eden to lie or to plead for mercy, but she refuses.

In a sick and twisted version of a swim meet, the people of Gilead watch as kettlebells are attached to Eden and Isaac's ankles.

The executioner also begs Eden to repent, but Eden just quotes the Bible. Nick and June look on in horror, and even Serena who is cradling a child that could meet this same fate, is crying. Eden's mother cries out her name.

And Eden and Isaac jump to their deaths, into a pool filled with kettleballs.

What a fucking place that kills children that they were so in need of to begin with.

Back in the kitchen, Rita is beating herself up over how terribly she treated Eden. June tries to comfort Nick, but he brushes her off. And when Nichole/Holly starts crying to be fed, Serena relents and allows June to breast feed.

Self-Care Suggestion:

Print out a picture of Fred and hang it on the wall and throw balled up socks at it. He is the worst. Calling Eden a slut for running away for love and then in the next breath trying to blackmail June into having sex with him in exchange for seeing Hannah again shows how corrupt and delusional he is.

Chapter Twenty-Three: Get in the Fucking Van, June

Season Two, Episode Thirteen: The Word
Season Finale

"Get in the fucking van, June. Just. Get. In. The.
Fucking. Van. June." ~ Me

Trigger Warnings: My blood pressure went straight through the roof
during the escape, very tense, taut and nail biting
Gut Punch Rating: 4
Favorite Quote: "Go fuck yourself, Fred."~June. *Seriously, I want*
this to be my ringtone.

It's the season finale and I'm wondering if we're going to end June's
story and pick up the next season with a new handmaid. Emily's
household is definitely more interesting than the Waterfords right
now. Fred and Serena have already won. They have baby Nichole,
and once June has stopped being a wet nurse for her own baby, she's
off to another assignment.

Or is she?

As June is packing up Eden's belongings, she finds a Bible—
with notes in it. Not only was Eden reading, she was writing. Now
that I try to do the timeline of Gilead in my head, she was probably
just out of kindergarten when it all started. It's possible that she had
just learned how to read and write before the world turned upside
down.

Makes you wonder if she really did read the handmaids' letters. I
don't think she did. I think she is so Gilead indoctrinated, she would
have turned Nick in—as a good wife would. And it's obvious that she
was willing to die for her convictions.

June storms into Serena's greenhouse to confront her about Eden's fate. Serena is bothered by this, but she shakily holds the Gilead line that Eden was a sinner.

She was 15 fucking years old. Even Serena isn't buying the Gilead bullshit. You can start to see cracks. And I don't want to like Serena! But like Aunt Lydia, she is a fantastic character.

June gasps out in agony that all Eden wanted to do was read God's word. What will happen if Nichole/Holly wants to do that? She's seen from Fred's reaction that Nichole/Holly will meet the same fate as Eden. Eden, who was born and raised in Gilead's world—or at least in enough of it that she can't remember any other way—was executed as a traitor. This does not bode well for any girl child of Gilead.

"How are you going to keep her safe?" June asks Serena.

Serena is shook by this, but rallies by saying her daughter will be "a good, God-fearing child who obeys his word."

"She cannot read his word," June laments, torn between rage and despair. If Eden could have this fate, what chance does Nichole/Holly have?

Afterwards, June is in Fred's study where she finds out that Eden and Isaac had run back to her family, and that it was her own father that turned her into the guardians. Fred is still butt hurt and tells the "grieving father" that Eden should be a lesson to his other daughter.

What a fucking prince among men.

When they're alone, June snarls at him, "What are you going to do when they come for *your* daughter?" Fred turns and locks the door. "Mind your tongue," he threatens and slaps her hard across the face.

Reeling from the blow, June rallies and does the unthinkable. She cracks him back.

No lie. I stood up and cheered.

"Your girlfriend is badass," Rita tells Nick afterwards.

But Fred is going to make June pay for that. One way or another.

On a brighter note, Nick gets a chance to hold his daughter for the first time.

June's words have affected Serena, and knowing that Nichole needs a better future in Gilead, she decides to start a mini revolution all on her own. The Bible is the word of God and should be shared with everyone. Wives should be allowed to read the Bible—at least according to Serena's viewpoint.

So she gathers up the wives and they agree to go visit the menfolk in their *very important* meeting space, which you know smells like old farts, bourbon and cigar smoke. Serena is so sure that they will allow them this small victory, that she doesn't even think about the consequences of a woman reading in Gilead.

At first their husbands share a strained smile and try to send the little women on their way, but then Serena opens up the Bible and starts to read from it. But this isn't America anymore and Fred isn't going to demand that she has a right to speak. Like Eden's father, he turns on her when she needed him the most.

Fred has to put Serena in her place to regain some of the power that he lost while he was in the hospital. That's why he allows the guards to haul her off to get her finger removed. After all, he beat her and she didn't listen. It's got to escalate, otherwise the wimmens get uppity.

Speaking of uppity wimmen, Emily tucks a knife up her sleeve as she prepares for the first ceremony in Commander Lawrence's house. Except, he's not interested and orders her back to her room.

Why did he request a handmaid—the world's worst handmaid—if not for procreation?

The next morning, Aunt Lydia stops by because her Auntie-senses are tingling. Commander Lawrence said the ceremony went well, but she isn't so sure. It's like she's looking for Emily to roll over on Lawrence. But when Emily doesn't say anything, Aunt Lydia snarls, "It's like I cut out your tongue." Instead of yanno—her clit.

Which got a bitch stabbed.

That's right. Emily does what I have wanted to do for two seasons. She stabs Aunt Lydia in the back and slaps her down the stairs.

This is a great episode for rage reactions.

I held my hand over my mouth. I wanted to stand up and cheer for this, but I was too afraid for Emily. Holy shit.

Emily knows it's a death sentence, but in that moment, she didn't care. She huddles in her room to await her fate.

Back at the Waterfords, Fred guides Serena through the door, shocked and defeated. "I tried," she whispers to June. June comforts her while Fred is really put out that Rita isn't there to make Mrs. Waterford her "I lost a pinkie" tea. He bemoans that all he wants is obedient women in his life. Is that so hard?

I rolled my eyes so hard I got eye strain.

"How could you let them do that to Serena?" June whispers.

"We all have our roles to play. Serena needed to be reminded of hers."

If looks could kill, Fred would be splattered all over the kitchen. You can tell if June had a knife he'd have gotten the "Aunt Lydia" treatment.

But Fred gets off on having the power to subjugate June and he either doesn't see the dangerous look in her eyes, or he's choosing to ignore it. "An obedient handmaid might be able to stay in this house. How does that sound?"

Barf.

"That's not allowed," June tells him.

"The rules can be bent for a high ranking commander." No shit.

He's been bending the rules left and right. The Orwellian *Animal Farm* mantra of "some animals are more equal than others" has got to be wearing thin with the other commanders. I mean for fuck's sake, Warren got his arm cut off for a blow job. There's got to be some disgruntled commanders who want to see Fred eat dirt.

"You can stay here," Fred oozes out like an oily sludge. "We can try again. For a boy this time. It could be fun."

He wants a child of his own. Not Nick's. And he wants a boy, not a troublesome girl. This doesn't bode well for the baby.

"Go fuck yourself, Fred."

YAS!

But instead of being mad or punching her out again, he says all sly, "Maybe I can arrange more visits with Hannah. As long as you behave properly. Think about it."

He's just bending all those Gilead rules for a chance to dip his wick. He knows June's weakness and will dangle Hannah like a carrot over her head for the rest of their lives.

Go fuck yourself, Fred.

Back in the Lawrence household, the Commander enters Emily's room where she is cowering by the bed. He croaks out, "What are we going to do with you?" The menace in the air is brittle; we've seen what happened for much lesser offenses. What gory new torture are the Aunts going to put poor Emily through now? She got the colonies for killing a guard. What can they do to her for killing (?) an Aunt?

Emily is beyond speech, but she manages to tell the Commander's wife—who is freaking out again—that it was nice knowing her, as Lawrence drags Emily to the car. Emily quietly sobs in the backseat while Lawrence puts on Annie Lennox's "Walkin' on Broken Glass." Emily just wants the games to end, though. She's been raped, mutilated, sent to the colonies. She asks him to turn off the radio.

"So, not a music fan," Lawrence says, bemused.

He's an odd duck. I can't place him. He's obviously profiting and thriving in Gilead, and yet he seems to love and care for his Bertha Rochester-esque wife, and has allowed a lot of leeway with a back talking Martha.

Back at the Waterfords, shit is going down. Dogs are barking. A fire has started. Along with the Marthas, Nick has arranged for June and baby Nichole/Holly to get out on the femaleroad. When Nick nods for her to go, June takes the baby and gets out.

Fred is suspicious and runs upstairs only to find that the baby is gone, and written in giant letters on the wall above the bed is *Nolite Te Bastardes Carborundorum*. I'm not sure what she used to write it with, but the look on Fred's face is priceless. Nick is right behind him with his gun and stops Fred from going after June.

But Serena is right behind her.

I figured it's all over that June is going to hang on the wall, probably right next to Emily. Fred and Serena will have their happily ever after and I'm about to flip tables and stomp around the house. But it seems Serena did learn a few things from her punishments, just not the lessons Gilead wanted to reinforce. No girl child is safe in Gilead.

And after holding her tearfully one last time, Serena lets the daughter of her heart escape with her real mother.

Not at all what I was expecting.

And the next harrowing 10 minutes is watching June run through the fields and back streets of Gilead, going from Martha to Martha.

No one escapes Gilead.

The dread is building up inside me. There's no way this will end

119

well, and yet, here we are again. Nick has sent June away with their baby. Is this season going to end like the book did? Nick, through his influence, has again put her in a van. This time, we know he's helping her escape, but as we've seen when June tried to get out the last time via airplane, it's not that easy. Are we still not going to learn the fate of June and her baby?

And what about Hannah? June is torn. How can she escape with one child and leave another behind?

And then, under the overpass, we see Emily with Commander Lawrence.

"God speed," he tells her.

"What is happening?" Emily cries out.

"I'm getting myself in deep shit," he answers. "Have a nice life. Don't get caught. Keep away from drugs."

Holy shit. Lawrence is one of the good guys.

Emily calls for June to hurry up and get in the fucking van. June just hands her the baby and tells her the baby's name is Nichole.

What the fuck? No, it's not. It's Holly. What are you fucking doing, June?

June closes the van's door and it takes off out of Gilead.

I can't even.

There is no way the Waterfords are going to explain this away. There is no way anyone is going to believe June didn't try to escape three times.

"Burning Down the House" by the Talking Heads plays as the credits roll.

Self-Care Suggestion:

Primal scream therapy. Scream into a pillow. And queue up Season Three, because what else can you do?

Season Two Reflections

The last episode in this series sent my blood pressure through the roof. I was genuinely surprised that Emily was on her way out of Gilead, and gobsmacked that June didn't go with her. The logic of it bothers me. She had to have known that going back to the Waterfords would be an instant trip to the wall for her. And yet June is banking hard that the Waterfords are going to cover for her to keep their own necks from stretching. It's a dangerous tight rope to walk.

I get why she did it. Hannah is still out there, vulnerable and alone. Hannah knows that she was taken from her family, and she knows that June didn't have a choice. She's a smart little girl, but she's also still just a child. I can't imagine how this is going to have a happy ending. It's like what George R.R. Martin said about his *Game of Thrones* series: "If you think this is going to end well, you haven't been paying attention."

However, June's decision goes back to the theme of the novel—or at least the theme that's been haunting me since childhood. For evil to flourish, good people just have to do nothing. Or in June's case, save herself and leave her first child behind to suffer. Then her small victory over Gilead would be meaningless. Sure, she saved Holly, but at the cost of Hannah. June would be haunted everyday that she hadn't at least tried to rescue her first daughter.

I'm not sure if it's courage or desperation, but June's got a lot of balls to think she can basically kidnap Hannah out of a commander's well-guarded home, let alone get across the border with her without any help from the Martha network or the underground femaleroad.

Season Two has turned the tide and we binge watchers are finally getting a little payback for the emotional investment we put in while watching Season One. Serena, in a confusing turn around, gives up the thing she's wanted more than anything else. I have to wonder what she thinks that's going to get her. Does she expect that they'll try again with another handmaid, one that's a little more pliable and will give them a boy this time? I don't want to like Serena, but she truly loves baby Holly/Nichole.

The kidnapped baby is probably going to play hell on Fred's career, and it couldn't happen to a nicer guy. Fuck you, Fred.

Do you think Aunt Lydia's dead? I don't think we're that lucky. Some things are just too mean and ornery to die. But I'd like to think the fall down the stairs and the knife in her back has taken away some of her confidence. I'm hoping she'll always feel that twinge where the knife went in and know that Gilead did not protect her. The handmaid that she abused had fought back. It wasn't an eye for an eye, or a clit for a clit in Emily's case. But it was the next crack of revolution that began with Lillie and her detonator.

And we have hope, something that was severely lacking in the first season.

Now, we know Mayday is real. They're serious and they have a network that is openly working to topple Gilead. It may be all "Praised Be" in the streets, but behind closed doors, it's on. It's slow going, but I guess revolutions always are.

I worry about Nick. Showing Fred the gun and forcing him indoors makes him culpable. He's just a driver, who may still be working as an Eye, but his protection is gone. How is Nick going to stay off the wall after this? He helped a handmaid escape. I'm wondering if it comes down to his word against theirs, if it's Gilead's policy just to hang them all and wash their hands of the entire mess. From Gilead's HQ point of view, Fred's household is a dumpster fire.

Serena denies everything, while. Fred tells the truth, the truth that June stole the baby and Nick held him hostage to give her time to escape. When June comes back, wouldn't it be her and Nick in the van going to Eye Headquarters for questioning? Or are they afraid that when the truth comes out, the Eye will rightfully hang them all on the wall together as one dysfunctional family?

No matter what happens in Season Three, though, Gilead is not doing well. They lost their trade agreement, their Canadian treaty, and now a handmaid and a baby. I'm not sure there is enough "Under his eye" that will cover up the stinking manure pile that is Gilead. And that gives me hope.

Hope for June and Hannah, but also for Trumpified America. Just like on the TV show, our allies are watching. Americans are slowly wakening up. They're waiting. And when the time is right, I'm hoping that the good guys will not stay home or take the easy route. I hope we fight. I hope we protest until the bad guys can no longer take it. I hope ripping down Confederate statues is just the beginning. I hope that arresting and prosecuting the murderers of black men and women will finally convince the nice/good people who don't like conflict and just want to live their lives that it's only "all lives matter" when Black Lives Matter.

Evil has been gaining a foothold in the past four years. We cannot be like pre-America Gilead and pretend that shit like this couldn't happen. It has happened. And it will happen, if good people choose to use their privilege to put their heads in the sand and wait it out, hoping it will all blow over so we can get back to our normal lives.

In 1946, Martin Niemoller gave a speech about this. You've probably heard it in some shape or form. This translation taken from Wikepedia (https://en.wikipedia.org/wiki/First_they_came_...) has alarming similarities to today's headlines.

"...the people who were put in the camps then were Communists. Who cared about them? We knew it, it was printed in the newspapers. Who raised their voice, maybe the Confessing Church? We thought: Communists, those opponents of religion, those enemies of Christians—"Should I be my brother's keeper?"

Then they got rid of the sick, the so-called incurables. I remember a conversation I had with a person who claimed to be a Christian. He said: Perhaps it's right, these incurably sick people just cost the state money, they are just a burden to themselves and to others. Isn't it best for all concerned if they are taken out of the middle [of society]? Only then did the church as such take note.

Then we started talking, until our voices were again silenced in public. Can we say, we aren't guilty/responsible?

The persecution of the Jews, the way we treated the occupied countries, or the things in Greece, in Poland, in Czechoslovakia or in Holland, that were written in the newspapers... I believe, we Confessing-Church-Christians have every reason to say: mea culpa, mea culpa! We can talk ourselves out of it with the excuse that it would have cost me my head if I had spoken out.

We preferred to keep silent. We are certainly not without guilt/fault, and I ask myself again and again, what would have happened, if in the year 1933 or 1934—there must have been a possibility—14,000 Protestant pastors and all Protestant communities in Germany had defended the truth until their deaths? If we had said back then, it is not right when Hermann Göring simply puts 100,000 Communists in the concentration camps, in order to let them die. I can imagine that perhaps 30,000 to 40,000 Protestant Christians would have had their heads cut off, but I can also imagine that we would have rescued 30–40,000 million [sic] people, because that is what it is costing us now."

"They came first for the Communists, and I didn't speak up because I wasn't a Communist. Then they came for the Jews, and I didn't speak up because I wasn't a Jew. Then they came for the trade unionists, and I didn't speak up because I wasn't a trade unionist. Then they came for the Catholics, and I didn't speak up because I was a Protestant. Then they came for me, and by that time no one was left to speak up."

~ Poem by Martin Niemoeller
at the Holocaust memorial in Boston MA

SEASON THREE

Chapter Twenty-Four: Burning Down the House

Season Three, Episode One: Night

"Yea, though I walk through the valley of the shadow of death,
I will fear no evil"
~ Psalm 23 King James Bible

Trigger Warnings: almost drowning
Gut Punch Rating: 2

Season Three picks up minutes after Season Two ends, and June is not leaving Gilead without her daughter Hannah. Luckily, it's Commander Lawrence who picks up June and drives her to Commander MacKenzie's house. As she sneaks up the stairs to take Hannah, she is struck with wanting her to wake up so as not to add to the poor kid's trauma.

When the guardians start to arrive, Lawrence takes off. June quickly ties a ribbon around Hannah's wrist before leaving the bedroom and kneeling down with her hands behind her head.

I'm surprised that the guards resist from hitting her in the face with the butt of their rifles. Are we seeing the kinder, gentler side of Gilead? It's off-putting after spending two seasons with the Waterfords.

The commander's wife seems like a decent sort—for a child stealing zealot—and she stops the guards from brutalizing June and dragging her out of the house. They talk about Hannah, her favorite things and how they both love her very much. It's uncomfortable. And in a horrific way, Mrs. MacKenzie makes good points. The least traumatic thing for Hannah—now renamed Agnes—is to let her forget June and her pre-Gilead life completely. Except, that really sucks because Gilead stole her from her rightful parents. And unfortunately in Gilead, that's completely legal.

127

Since June has no good way of taking Hannah/Agnes by force, there's not a lot she can do. She can't live with her in Gilead, taking her from household to household, as she's raped by commander after commander. There's just no way to keep her daughter with her and no way to escape Gilead with her...at the moment. Hannah/Agnes is safe where she is.

"She's very happy here," Mrs. MacKenzie says. "She's thriving." The last time she saw June, Hannah had nightmares and woke up screaming for weeks. "This has to end." Mrs. MacKenzie tells June.

June is in a tough place and her future is on tether hooks. She doesn't want to cause Hannah any more trauma. If June's not heading for the Colonies, she's heading for the wall once Gilead catches her for giving Holly/Nichole to Emily. So just like Serena did, June decides to give up her child because, for right now, it's best for her. Not that she had much of a choice. And at least she has the small comfort that Mrs. MacKenzie is not Serena.

June's once again taken back to the Waterfords while Fred tries to come up with another story that will keep them all off the wall. Nick is told to escort June to her room, which is really against Gilead's rules, but in the grand scheme of what happened tonight I suppose that's nitpicking. But he has the gall to call her selfish for not escaping with Nichole.

Fuck you, Nick.

It's not selfish for wanting to save your child. She saved yours. Now, she's back to save hers. I mean, I get it. A lot of Martha's and Mayday rebels risked their lives to get her and the baby out. But no one asked June if she was willing to leave without her daughter. How could she live with herself?

I think Nick and June's romance won't survive this and I'm not sure that's a good thing. I can't see this battle forged June settling for sweet Luke. Nick and June have the shared trauma and I think they're going to need each other, but this isn't a romance novel, and to quote George RR Martin about his own books, "If you think there's going to be a happy ending, you haven't been paying attention."

In the end, Fred decides to blame it all on Emily, claiming that she stole the child when she escaped. This might be more believable if June wasn't known for running away. But so far, the lies are working—mostly because no one wants to look too closely. This might be a show of Fred's power in Gilead, or it might be Gilead worried about showing that the rebellion has enough power to "steal" children.

Serena, however, is still not all right after willingly letting the baby go. Everything that she has ever done in her life was to have a baby, and after she got what she wanted, she let her go. She let her go, because the horror show of a government that she helped create made it so girl babies are not safe. Granted, she thought she was letting the baby go with June, whom she trusted to care for her because June's her real mother. But now, "her" baby will be raised by strangers—just like Hannah/Agnes is.

For the first time, Serena feels what other women in Gilead feel and it's not sitting too well with her. Serena sets the house on fire, starting with the bed Nichole was conceived in.

June manages to escape with Serena from the burning house, but she won't be going back to the Waterfords. Her and Nick exchange a farewell glance. It's still a little chilly, but maybe there will be another time for them.

Emily on the other hand, is running as fast as she can to Canada. When she crosses a raging river, the baby goes underwater for a long time. When they finally make it to shore, Holly/Nichole doesn't make a sound for several agonizing seconds.

I'm in shock. No. You can't kill a baby. Not this baby. Not now.

But this is not a show that shies away from horrific scenes. And just when I think they're going to go there, the baby cries. Emily's tears of anguish turn to relieved sobs. Soon, she's confronted by border patrol and, cowering, she can't quite realize that she's safe.

Unlike how the United States treat refugees seeking asylum, the border guards in Canada offer Emily sanctuary and respect.

"Do you wish to seek asylum in the country of Canada?" he asks her kindly.

It's hard to trust a man with a uniform and a gun, but he's not hitting her or touching her.

Emily nods, still wary. But her bravery is rewarded, and she is wrapped up in one of those aluminum thermal blankets and taken to safety. Emily and baby are free from Gilead's clutches. They're brought to a hospital staff of all female doctors and nurses, and as Emily passes through the halls, they applaud and cheer for her.

Back in Gilead, June is brought back to The Red Center where her feet are whipped and she's forced to do manual labor. It's surprisingly anti-climactic after what we've seen. But her "only" crime was running off to see her real daughter and bothering the MacKenzies. Since there's no reason for her to go back to the Waterfords, and Fred hasn't made good on his threat to try for a boy ::shudder::, June's taken to her new assignment. She's the Handmaid for Commander Lawrence. June is now Ofjoseph.

"You aren't going to give me trouble, are you?" Lawrence asks.

"No sir," June replies sweetly.

Yeah, right.

If Aunt Lydia managed to survive, she's going to shit a brick sideways. There's no way she's dead. Some things are just too mean and hate filled to die. Aunt Lydia is one of them.

Self-Care Suggestion:

The awful things that almost happened in this episode, kept me waiting for the other shoe to drop. Like trying to prepare yourself for the jump scare in horror movies. Close this stress circle by watching a horror movie or a suspenseful whodunit movie where there's an ending and closure in two hours. We're a long time to getting closure with this series, but at least things are looking up.

Chapter Twenty-Five: Give 'Em the Old Razzle Dazzle

Season Three, Episode Two: Mary and Mother

"Strange to finally be invisible. One of the reasons they chose red was the opposite. We're easy to catch because we're easy to see. Like blood on the snow." ~June

Trigger Warnings: blood, death, just a typical day in the neighborhood
Gut Punch Rating: 2
Favorite Quote: "That must have been some blowjob."~Beth
"Red Center Special."~June

Ofmatthew, June's new walking partner, tells June that her mistress says that Gilead is about to take back Chicago. Of course, she also tells June that she's praying for the Waterfords.

"What could Ofjoseph been thinking?" Ofmatthew smirks.

"I'm Ofjoseph," June says with her simple sweet tone that she only uses for the real pious assholes.

It shuts Ofmatthew right the hell up. Meanwhile, in the canned tomato section, Ofrobert (Alma) and June have a Mayday meeting. June is feeling emboldened, and wants to give her all to the resistance.

But back home at the Lawrences, Aunt Lydia has come to call. Told you she was still alive! They meet in the parlor.

"Lydia's come to check up on us," Lawrence says. I love that he doesn't call her "Aunt."

The meeting is short. Aunt Lydia asks about the ceremony and the Lawrences lie about it. I also love his flippant responses to the Gilead-isms. An "Under his eye" gets a grunt or a "Sure." This time he says that the ceremony went fine, "Aces." Mrs. Lawrence, whose

131

name is Eleanor, does not want to be there, though, and the Commander escorts her back to her bedroom.

Aunt Lydia feigns concern about the household, trying to get June to dish, but June's too smart for that. But she is at least more convincing than Emily was. Aunt Lydia, like everyone else, can't figure Commander Lawrence out. He has too much power in Gilead to have her throw her weight around, and she can't cow him like she does with Serena. But her Auntie senses are tingling that something is up and she wants to inspect June's bedroom. I guess to make sure it doesn't have a television, or phone or something in it.

She is having a hard time moving around, and when June tries to help her when she falls, Aunt Lydia freaks out and cattle prods June. Yanno, just in case she gets any hair-brained ideas that Emily weakened her, even if she's unable to stand.

"After what you pulled with the MacKenzies, you should be on the wall," Aunt Lydia rages. It's not like her to lose her shit like this. Emily must have really shaken her to the core with just how vulnerable an older woman is in Gilead.

The commander immediately comes back down the stairs, and Aunt Lydia says that June was gossiping at Loaves and Fishes.

"Spare the rod, and spoil the Handmaid," Lawrence says laconically. "I wonder what the voltage is on that thing."

I can't figure Lawrence out. On the one hand, his own wife calls him a monster and hates him for what he's done in creating Gilead. And he obviously holds a great deal of power. On the other hand, he has no interest in the ceremony and even helped Emily escape. But he definitely has his mood swings, especially in this episode. In Toronto, he'd be all bark and no bite, but here in Gilead, no woman could count on him not following up on his anger through something heinous. So it leaves them on pins and needles around him, wondering how much they can push their luck. And I think he gets off on that, the same way Fred got off playing Scrabble with June.

Speaking of Toronto, Luke is gathering information on Waterford while Moira is playing with Nichole. He's distancing himself from the baby, and wondering why Emily doesn't just contact her family, but Moira, tells him that everyone heals differently. And she and their roommate Erin make sure that he's going to be at dinner with Emily that night.

Coincidentally, Emily is at the doctor. Her ear is healing nicely, but it will probably scar from where Gilead put the handmaid cuff on it. She gets more doctor referrals—one for a clitoris reconstruction and another for a psychologist—but the most pressing concern in her checkup was her cholesterol. She spent months in the colonies, yet her biggest health concern is eating too much red meat and butter. Both anti-climatic and a relief at the same time.

Back at the Lawrence residence, the Marthas don't trust June. One-eyed Cora is there with Beth, who is also a cook at Jezebels. She was the one that was trying to fatten Nick up with her award winning Italian cooking.

The third Martha's name is Alison, who used to be a high school chemistry teacher. They're trying to get someone out of Gilead, even though Cora is against it because it's too dangerous. When the Commander walks in on their "hen party" looking for his wife's tea, he asks them what Alison is doing there. Cora tells him that she's there to polish the silver, but he quickly calls Cora out on the lie. He doesn't like strangers in his house and he doesn't like lies. He says he's going to call a guardian to escort her home. June goes after him and asks him to let the Martha escape.

"Okay," he says. "It's your funeral."

Psyched, June goes back in and demands to be a part of this, to which Beth reluctantly agrees and they're off, leaving Cora to watch the house. June is exhilarated to be out dressed like a Martha. She's invisible, but walking through the industrial part of Gilead is still fraught with checkpoints and danger. They drop off Alison and tell her to wait for someone to come for her.

On the way back, Beth and June bond. Beth apologizes for being a snarky bitch and June tells her that Moira, aka Ruby from Jezebels, escaped. Beth shares that Alison isn't escaping, but rather that she's going deeper into Gilead because she's a bomb maker.

Switching scenes to Canada, Luke is drunker than drunk and tries to figure out why Emily wouldn't reunite with her wife. He has to be wondering if June would hide from him too. Moira gets it, of course, because she's been through it. She knows that everything has changed, and it's been over three years since Emily has seen her wife Sylvia and their son.

"Nobody's talking about happily ever after. Just after," Moira says.

Back in Gilead, there's a knock on the door. Alison is back and she's been shot. They bring her down to the basement when Commander Lawrence hears the commotion and asks Cora what's going on.

"Who's in the basement?"

"No one," Cora says. "Just Beth. We saw a rat."

"Liar," he says. "That's two."

Lawrence knows more than he's letting on and when June tells him the truth, he orders her to get Alison out.

There's a bloody handprint on the wall, guardians at the door, and June tries to convince him to let the woman stay. June furiously tries to clean up the blood while Eleanor saves the day, coming down and asking the men for coffee. Suddenly, Mrs. Lawrence seems lucid and smart. What's this all about? She tells Cora to clean the wall and sends June back to the basement.

Beth wants to give Alison over to the guardians, but June says no way. They'll get her to talk and the whole network will be compromised. And unfortunately, Alison dies in the basement.

"This is why we don't move people," Beth says.

The Commander comes down and dismisses Beth, seeing the dead woman. "I was wrong. It was not your funeral after all. Women like you are like children, asking for too much, taking whatever you want. Damn the consequences."

He doesn't seem angry, just annoyed. But then June asks him how Mrs. Lawrence is holding up and he explodes like a grenade.

"Do not presume to speak to me about my wife!" Then in a quieter voice he says, "I knew it was a mistake taking you in."

He then orders her to clean up the mess. June digs a grave to put Alison in, while Lawrence watches from a window. Covered in dirt and sweat, June says a prayer over the fresh grave. Later, as she's soaking in the tub, Beth brings some medicine for June's hands. She tells her that Lawrence sent Cora away. He doesn't like liars. Turns out, Commander Lawrence is just as fucked up as the other Commanders. So much for June's easy life.

Back in Canada, baby Nichole is having a fussy night and Moira talks with Luke about how everyone is fucked up, and that it's okay. Moira mentions she remembers when Hannah was as small as Nichole. And it's then that Luke takes the baby and rocks her.

"June went back to save her, because I couldn't," he says. I'm getting a little annoyed with his fragile ego, but I'm willing to cut him some slack here.

Meanwhile, Ofmatthew is nattering on about the Martha who was trying to escape and how she hoped that when they catch her, they'll take her eye or maybe her ears for being so ungrateful. She had a purpose, and a home and safety. Why would anyone give that up?

I don't know what Ofmatthew is smoking, but June is having none of her nonsense. She remarks that it was such a shame what happened to Ofjohn. Her shopping partner snapped and pushed her in front of a bus. Of course, June says this just as a large bus goes by in front of them. Ofmatthew's eyes almost pop out of her head.

Back in Canada, Emily finally calls her wife. Sylvia doesn't even bother to pull the car over when she hears Emily's voice. She stops the car in the middle of traffic.

Self-Care Suggestion:

June is in a safer place, but she's not out of the woods yet. She's going to need all her skills to outsmart this commander and keep herself off the wall while she tries to find a way to escape with Hannah. If you're still feeling a little scattered, and I definitely was after the last two seasons, I found it helpful to do something creative, but also simple. Download a coloring page and break out the markers, crayons or colored pencils. I find it soothing to see the colors and the picture pop out. It helps me get my thoughts in order, which is what June is going to need in the episodes ahead.

Chapter Twenty-Six: Snark and Banter

Season Three, Episode Three: Useful

"You seem like you'd be good at making friends. Influencing people. Good at intimacy." ~ Commander Lawrence

"Thank you." ~ June

"Does this really work on Fred? Not exactly an intellectual giant. Then again, neither are you" ~ Commander Lawrence

"Perhaps you don't know me well enough, yet. Sir." ~June

"Here's what I don't get. If women don't want to be defined by their bodies, why are they always using them to get what they want?" ~Commander Lawrence

"Maybe they aren't. Maybe men are just too easily distracted." ~ June

Trigger Warnings: Hangings, reminder of Serena's loss of a finger, Lawrence being an ass, Fred being creepy.
Gut Punch Rating: 0 Things are mellowing out this season. Or I'm numb to it. I can't tell.
Favorite Quote: "You will get through this, by his hand."~Rita
"What's left of it."~Serena, looking down at her missing pinkie.

June wonders if Cora is swinging from the scaffolds in the square. She doesn't want to believe Lawrence would do that, but she's not sure. She knows she's going to have to make some powerful friends to survive. The new Martha's name is Sienna and Lawrence is already barking at and taunting her.

Today, the commanders are visiting Lawrence, and he's in a rare

137

mood. No one is safe from his menacing wit and vague questions that sound like threats. June tries to eavesdrop on the conversation, while Fred tries to pretend he wasn't looking for her. She butters him up, while trying to pump him for information about Lawrence.

Fred is not a big help. He tells her that Lawrence is a survivor, but he's also an enigma. He goes on to say that Lawrence doesn't like to be bored. "But I think you knew that already."

Lawrence, however, knows exactly what's going on and he comes into break it up.

While the commanders are having their muckety muck meeting about bringing in new girls from Chicago (I guess they managed to take it after all), Serena is at her mother's house by the ocean. Serena is living apart from Fred, which is about as close to divorce as you can get in Gilead. It's clear that Serena gets her stone-cold bitch from her mother, who basically tells her that there is no place in this world for her without Fred. And that she shouldn't be mourning a child that was never hers—especially since she gave it away.

Back in Gilead, Sienna tells June that Lawrence wants her to serve the drinks to the other commanders. June's not sure why, but she's pretty sure it's not because Sienna isn't pouring fast enough. So June goes into the lounge and overhears them talking about training centers and troop surges in Chicago. And holy shit... Nick is there.

Lawrence is watching June with interest. I think he knows all about who Nichole's father is. And Fred is watching Nick. Lawrence must think having June pour is much less boring than having Sienna do it. As they quibble about the troops needed to squash the remaining insurgents in Chicago, and about the fertile women and children there, Lawrence tells them to move on to the next thing on the agenda. It's about district-wide salvaging of women under the sway of terrorists. They were supposed to go to the colonies, but some commanders think they should just be killed instead.

Lawrence pipes up that there are uses for women and he calls June out while she's pouring the wine. He brings up that she used to be a book editor and asks if there are many books on the subject of gender and intelligence. She tells him there are. He bids her to get a book for him from the shelf—*The Dissent of Man*. It's a trick. If she reads the spine, she could lose a finger, but he quickly tells her it's a yellow book on the right. Fred and Nick are watching her with trepidation, while the others eagerly wait to see what's going to happen. She plays it right until he gives her better direction.

"Good job," he says.

She kneels in front of him and hands over the book. He dismisses her. "See," he jokes to the commanders. "Women can be useful."

June seethes.

Later, Fred gives a moving speech to cajole and persuade Serena to come back to him. It's a pretty good one. Unfortunately, he's practicing at Jezebels with a female psychologist.

"That sounds good," she says. "You want to run through it again?"

At the Lawrences', June decides to seduce Lawrence. She's not proud of herself, but she sees it as a way to regain control. She brings him some tea and tries to get him to talk. But Lawrence scorns her attempts to get under his skin and manipulate him. They have an honest, if adversarial conversation, which is both refreshing and scary. Lawrence is so much smarter than Fred. So much more dangerous. Fred's a thug and Lawrence is a tactician.

"Fred got demoted. Serena got defingered. The baby got baby napped. You left the place literally in ashes. How could they not see how contractual you are?"

"I did what I had to do," June says.

"You think that if you get me to like you, I'll help you."

"I think that you'd try to do the right thing." She tells him that she knows he helped Emily escape and that he lets the Marthas run a resistance ring out of his house.

But Lawrence demurs. He's not a good man, doing the right thing. "You have to let the rabble rousers blow off steam, otherwise they'll tear things to bits."

June tells him she thinks he feels guilty and this is his way of easing that guilt.

He tells her she was a fool for not getting on that truck with Emily. He saved Emily because she was brilliant and can help the world. The same way he is helping the world by replenishing it for the next generation—for Hannah.

Lawrence tells her that Mrs. Mackenzie is a better mother for Agnes than June. Mrs. Mackenzie sent fruit baskets to orphans in

Africa—when there used to be orphans. All June ever did was steal someone's husband and edit esoteric useless books instead of picking up her sick daughter from school. Yeah, not only does Lawrence know everything about June, he's not afraid to poke her in the feels about her past.

"You wrote those esoteric books," June says, rallying. "It must have been terrifying seeing those numbers turn into people, real people being executed." She hits the mark on him when she says, "If no one had read your books, we wouldn't be here right now. That's much worse than being useless."

When he starts to lose control of the argument, when June starts getting too close to the truth, he stands up and tells her she's awarding him too much humanity. And then he orders her to go for a drive with him. You can bet your ass they're not going to Jezebels. He doesn't even bother hiding her in his wife's clothes or dress her up like a Martha. While there are checkpoints, no one dares stops his car.

He leads June to a warehouse of cages with people stuffed in them like cattle. Lawrence tells her there will be no salvagings. They're all going to the colonies.

June notes that they're still going to die. It's just going to take longer.

Then Lawrence tells her she can save five of them to work as Marthas. Five out of hundreds. He'll give her everyone's dossiers so she can choose the best people for the job, but June refuses. Lawrence tells her to be useful for once. When she refuses again, he asks, "What if I tell you if you don't choose, they all die." June fights tears and tells him that he would be at fault, that Gilead would.

Later on that evening Nick stops by the Lawrence house, but it's not to see Beth or her fine Italian food. It's to see June. He tells her that he's being deployed to Chicago, the front, and that he's come to say goodbye. I guess Fred's getting his revenge by promoting him to Commander and sending him into a warzone.

"Goodbye," she tells him heartlessly, before running after him to brings him back to her room.

I'm wondering if there's a chance Nick will get her pregnant a second time.

The next day, Serena visits to talk about Nichole. June is a popular chick. Serena is falling apart, but June tries to get her as an ally because at least she's a woman. The men hate them. June tells her that they are stronger then they think they are.

The next day, June hands Lawrence the five names that will become Marthas: an engineer, a lawyer, an IT specialist, a journalist, and a thief. In a twist of Irony, she's become the activist that her mother wanted her to be.

And Serena walks into the ocean, but stops at waist height. I wouldn't mind seeing her drown here. It might be too easy of a death for her, but I'd accept it as her redemption arc. But like Aunt Lydia being too tough of a bitch to die, so is Serena. Turning back, she pulls herself out of the water. Fred's on the beach, but she walks right by him.

Self-Care Suggestion:

What would you have done if you were given a choice to save five people from sure death? Would you have told Lawrence to shove it or would you have chosen five? I would have chosen five, because at least I could strengthen the Martha network. I think June's choices are interesting. If you're feeling restless, you're not alone. Lawrence and June are playing a weird game of mind fucks. While I love to listen to them banter, Lawrence is too powerful for the game to be fun for either of them. And yet, he pushes June to watch her reaction.

Write in a journal today, just a few sentences or if you're inspired keep going. Write down what type of traits a female revolutionary would need to have to overthrow Gilead. Let's pretend that we're part of the plot to orchestrate Gilead's downfall.

Chapter Twenty-Seven: The Beatings Will Continue

Season Three, Episode Four: God Bless the Child

"We come together in peace to celebrate the babies born in our district. We dedicate ourselves and our children to God. It takes a village—and machine guns. Who among them can be persuaded? Who can be turned, ignited to burn this shit place to the ground?" ~ *June*

Trigger Warnings: Aunt Lydia lashing out like a wounded animal, Janine being painfully earnest.
Gut Punch Rating:1
Favorite Quote: "Have I missed anything?" ~ Serena
"Oh, just the usual. Jello shots. Charades. A little karaoke." ~ June

The episode starts with bells ringing and an orderly march of handmaids, Marthas, and Econowives, each filing in color coordinated and segregated order into the church/auditorium for baby Angela's baptism. June and Janine get priority seating for the event in front, while the Gilead mothers are on stage.

Aunt Lydia is flitting around on her scooter. "Hell on wheels," as Alma snarks.

We find out that June's pious little shit of a shopping partner, Ofmatthew, has had three children taken away from her and she's pregnant with the fourth one.

"I'm so blessed to serve," Ofmatthew says with a slight kink in her Pro-Gilead armor as doubt, grief, and regret briefly flash across her face.

And of course, the priest/religious leader conducting the shit show on stage makes sure that everyone prays for "the innocent child who was stolen from us, taken by an unrepentant sinner."

Fred looks at June.

143

June flashes back to Hannah's baptism where her mother Holly is being difficult in the church, calling it a place of "holier than thou child molesters." Moira gleefully snickers that they're not too happy that she's the "fairy" godmother of the child.

After the Gilead ceremony, Naomi Putnam brings everyone over to her palatial house—with an indoor swimming pool—to celebrate. Even the handmaids are allowed to come, which is not something that's usually done. Ofmatthew is very uncomfortable with this chain of events. In the van Aunt Lydia is in obvious pain, but when June asks how she's feeling, she tells June to watch out for herself. She then tells Janine to be a good girl and make her proud. And since Janine is eager to please Aunt Lydia, she agrees.

Serena makes an appearance at the reception for "Naomi's sake" since being at the actual ceremony would be too painful for her. June and Serena get some more time to talk about Nichole, and Serena asks if she regrets not leaving with the baby. June simply replies not without Hannah too.

It's like Serena has had a disconnect, that the same thing she's feeling right now happened to June and Luke. Only it was a hundred times worse because Hannah was old enough to understand what was going on. So Hannah hurt like Serena is hurting now. Except Serena is too self-centered to see that what she is feeling, is what every handmaid feels when they give up their child. June tells Serena that she has hope that one day she'll see Hannah again and Serena says, "I can't say the same thing about Nichole."

Oh, I'm pretty sure if you took Mark, the American agent, up on his offer to defect to Hawaii you could see Nichole again.

Fred spots them talking and makes a beeline for them. I don't blame you, Fred. Last time you left the two of them alone, they ran Gilead for a couple of weeks.

But Serena isn't ready to reconcile with him yet and walks right by his outstretched hand to greet Naomi and baby Angela instead.

Back in Canada, Emily is reunited with her wife Sylvia, and their son Oliver. It's awkward, sad and sweet at the same time. Sylvia bought Emily's favorite tea—the one that tastes like dirt. Emily wonders if Oliver even remembers her, but when Sylvia takes her into his room it's covered with pictures of them. One is even a colored picture of Emily as a superhero, fighting to get back home.

When Oliver does show up, he says, "I'm not supposed to hug you until you're ready." And Emily's heart melts a little and says that they can wait until they're both ready.

"He's so big!" she mouths at Sylvia, and Sylvia says, "I know."

Back in Gilead, Aunt Lydia is stalking around alone. She groans as she takes a seat. Janine brings her tea.

"I prayed so hard for you to get better," Janine says with her sweet smile. "We all did."

"I'm sure." Aunt Lydia snorts. "I know what the girls think of me."

And rightly so.

The other Handmaids can't figure out why Janine thrives on affection from Aunt Lydia.

"She's doing her best," Ofmatthew says, defending Aunt Lydia.

"Did she burn you, breeder?" Alma replies, showing her arm where Aunt Lydia held it over a flame because Alma wouldn't stone Janine to death.

Fred interrupts the handmaids and it takes him no time at all to scatter them to the deviled eggs at the buffet so he can ask June how to get his wife back.

What the fuck? Like they're friends.

It's obvious that he wants her back because he's losing face with the good old boys in the bourbon brigade.

June thought something really icky when she saw him. She doesn't hate him. "It's not love," she thought. "It's more complicated." Jesus June, tell him whatever lies you have to in order to survive, but don't start believing this shit. He's evil incarnate and doesn't deserve anything but a firing squad.

She's not above manipulating him, though and tells him if he gives Serena a little bit of power—no one has to know—things might get back to normal.

Fred oozes that that might not be completely out of the question. "It's worth discussing, but she hasn't said two words to me." Yeah, that's what happens when you let thugs drag your screaming wife out of sight and let them chop off her pinkie.

But June's on the case, and. she finds Serena smoking by the pool. Ugh, shades of Eden. She lays it out for Serena and begs her to "wear the dress, but pull the strings."

145

Serena hands her a cigarette and they smoke in quiet, comfortable silence. I don't get this tentative friendship at all.

Back in Canada, Emily tries to read a bedtime story to Oliver, but as soon as he cuddles up to her as if the past several years never happened, she and Sylvia start to cry. For Oliver, it's as simple as his mom is back. But Emily knows she's not the same person, and the trauma of wondering if Sylvia and Oliver would still love her if they knew what she had done eats at her. She's like a dreamer, expecting to wake up and be back in the colonies again.

Afterwards, she shares a beer on the porch with her wife, deciding to spend time with her instead of running back to her hotel room. It's a start.

Back at the Putnam baptismal extravaganza, things have been going too well and Janine asks to hold the baby. Cue the horrified silence, but Naomi is gracious and allows Janine to hold baby Angela, who starts to cry as she feels that Naomi is her mother. I expected Janine to snap, but she surprised all of us—even cattle prodding Aunt Lydia who had moved in for the kill. She hands the baby back without incident and everyone—especially me—gives a sigh of relief.

But then Janine has to ruin it, by asking if they want Angela to have a brother or a sister.

Aunt Lydia lunges in.

"I just want to be with my daughter," Janine whimpers.

See, Serena?

Aunt Lydia beats Janine savagely with her cane, shouting, "No" over and over again until June throws her body over Janine. I'm not sure why that stops Aunt Lydia. After all, June is no longer pregnant. Is it because she's frightened of Commander Lawrence, who has already seen her cattle prod June recently?

Something brings Aunt Lydia around and she apologies to the horrified Commanders and wives. I'm not sure what they're so surprised about. I guess things like that are best done in privacy at the Rachel and Leah Center, and not front and center in the middle of a baptism party. How gauche, Lydia.

"My deepest apologies," Aunt Lydia says, before going off to another room to break down into sobs. Her optics can't be looking good. She brought Emily back from the colonies, who then stole a baby and got the better of Aunt Lydia in a fight. It made her look weak. Then June was assigned to Commander Lawrence, instead of going on the wall where Aunt Lydia would have put her.

Aunt Lydia is losing power.

And if the Aunts are any bit like the wives and the Econowives, they sense weakness and offer the prey up to the predator to save themselves. Aunt Lydia's days in Gilead could very well be numbered. The cracks are beginning to show.

Aunt Lydia's scene was definitely a party stopper and as everyone is getting ready to leave, Serena whispers in June's ear where Hannah goes to school. But when she turns around to thank her, Serena has disappeared. However, a guardian comes in looking for Fred and June risks the Aunt Lydia special by following him to eavesdrop.

He has footage of Luke holding Nichole at a protest to free Chicago.

Serena is smitten again. She wanted to see Nichole again, and now she has. And now she wants her back. Uh-oh. The guardian has June identify Luke and leaves the Waterfords, while she sinks to the floor outside and cries. On the one hand, Luke and Nichole are safe and happy. On the other, she's still in Gilead and now the Waterfords know how to reach them.

Self-Care Suggestion:

Protest is a good thing. Be like Luke and baby Nichole and do something that will further your politics. Write a letter to your Congressperson or representative. Volunteer for voter registration or to help out at the polls. Get involved in a lobbyist group. Make your voice heard. It feels good to be proactive and doing something. It helps with the worry a bit.

Chapter Twenty-Eight: What about Hannah?

Season Three, Episode Five: Unknown Caller

"She's out. She's safe. She's with Luke.... I want to be held and told my name. If I thought I'd never touch him, I'd die. But it's not for lack of sex, it's for lack of love." ~ June

Trigger Warnings: Betrayal, Serena reverting to type, Fred being Fred, Poor Luke—all the feels for Luke.

Gut Punch Rating: 2

Favorite Quote: "Blessed day, Commander."~June

"The answer is no. You want something. I can tell." ~Commander Lawrence

"I just need to know if my husband is safe."~June

"I don't know. Does he use a seat belt? Does he watch his blood pressure? That's the silent killer, you know." ~Commander Lawrence

Serena is back. And not in a good way. Seeing Nichole with Luke last episode really did a number on her. She doesn't like that her baby is with him, whether it's because he's black, because he does manual labor, or if it's just that Nichole is not with her mother, she's determined to get her back.

Fred brings her into an important man meeting where the Gilead government drones debrief her on Nichole's status, and that they're doing everything in their power to get her back. But since there isn't an extradition treaty with Canada, it's going to be difficult. After the drones leave, Fred asks Serena, "I thought this is what you wanted. Our child safe in Canada."

She says, "I want to be with her, but I can't. So I want this to be over."

149

Fred has a bright idea how June can help them with all that.

Meanwhile, back at the Lawrences', Commander Lawrence is desperately in love with his wife, but she just can't forgive him for everything he's done. June manages to put in her mind that maybe there's some of her old love left in him. Eleanor mentions that he used to make her mixed tapes and that they're in the basement.

"It's okay to take a sliver and hold on to that, especially if that's all you have," June tells her.

The Waterfords show up and Fred announces his insane plan that June should help them arrange a visit with Serena and Nichole to say goodbye. They assure her that Luke would be protected. June of course refuses, but when Serena presses and appeals to June's maternal emotions, June relents. But only if Serena now owes her a favor. June is all in with the resistance and is willing to sell her soul to see Gilead fall.

In an excruciating two minutes, June—who hasn't spoken to her husband in over three years—has to convince Luke to bring Nichole to the Toronto airport to meet Serena.

How can anyone trust Gilead to keep their promise to keep Luke safe? Has she just handed Nichole and Luke to Gilead? Will she have to see Luke swinging on the wall?

After the call, Commander Lawrence offers her a handkerchief, but June coldly asks if she is dismissed. He lets her go.

Moira later asks Luke, "How did she sound?"

"She sounded like June," he says helplessly.

At her mother's house, Serena is packing things for Nichole, like a creepy medallion that says, "For this child I prayed." Rita asks Serena to give the baby a kiss for her and hands her a package that arrived last night.

Is Serena now a part of Mayday?

Serena flies into Toronto alone, at Luke's request. Mark is waiting for her there with a change of clothes so she doesn't scream Gilead in her blue outfit.

"God bless you," Serena says to Luke when she sees him.

"Fuck you," Luke replies.

It doesn't get much better from there. Luke manages to get Serena to tell him which commander is raping his wife, but he doesn't ask about his daughter. That's what's puzzling me. Why didn't Luke make it a condition of this meeting?

You can see "your" daughter, when I can see mine.

Oh, "your" daughter was stolen?

Mine too.

Why aren't the Americans/Canadians hitting back with the fact that Hannah has been ripped away from her family? Why didn't he ask Serena about his daughter? It makes me mad at Luke.

In the end, after Serena throws out that she protected June (literally leaving out the fact that she goaded her husband into raping June days before Nichole's birth) and by virtue that she obviously loves Nichole, Luke lets her hold the baby.

Big fucking mistake, Luke.

Although, I think what happens next would have happened anyway.

Mark tells Serena that his offer still stands, but Serena tells him she only has one home. But she does give him the package that says "For Luke."

Back in Gilead, Eleanor and Lawrence are listening to one of the mixed tapes he made her. "Cruel to be Kind" by Nick Lowe plays as June watches them.

Serena tells Fred that Nichole is perfect and leans into him for support saying, "This is so hard."

"It doesn't have to be."

Fred is up to something.

June and Ofmatthew are walking to market. Ofmatthew seems off and it turns out that she's uneasy about her pregnancy, and uncharacteristically says that she's glad Nichole and June's husband are safe.

At the market, the guardians have come for June and they put her in the back of the van. What? Why? What have they found out?

Back in Canada, a mixed tape was in the package for Luke. He puts it in, and instead of music, it's June's voice. She recorded over the songs to tell him everything she wanted to and couldn't in their two-minute phone call.

She tells him that she had to build a life in Gilead and she wants him to build one too, that she will always love him. June tells him that Nichole's real name is Holly and her father was Nick—the guy you met in the bar.

"I'm doing what I need to do to survive. It's all for Hannah. I promise you. I'm trying to get to her."

151

At least one of Hannah's parents care enough to work for her release. I'm still mad at Luke.

Back in Gilead, after June's van ride, Aunt Lydia is waiting for her with a formal handmaid's outfit.

"Lucky girl," Aunt Lydia says with some of her old acidic vim and vigor.

June gets walked out to a sound stage that's set up to look like the Waterford's house.

"What did you do?" she mutters to Serena.

"Don't think about being clever," Aunt Lydia warns.

The Waterfords make a video pleading with the world to force Canada to send Nichole back.

June glares into the screen, fists clenched.

Luke is now a target.

Self-Care Suggestion:

Fred and Serena deserve each other. You know what they don't deserve? That baby. I hope Luke, Moira, and the rest of team Little America can keep her safe from these sociopaths. Light a candle or some sage to get the stench of bullshit out of the air. Bonus points if you can get one that has a flickering wick that sounds like a crackling fire. That way you can remember fondly the Waterfords' house burning to the ground.

Chapter Twenty-Nine: Tell Me How You Really Feel, June

Season Three, Episode Six: Household

"This isn't love. You can't love! You don't know how! Serena, you built this whole world just so that you can have someone. But it didn't work. You're small. You're cruel. And you're empty. You will always be empty."~June

"I should have put a ring in your mouth the day that we met."~Serena

"I should have let you burn when I had the chance."~June

Trigger Warnings: OMG the silenced Handmaids, You thought Massachusetts was bad? Wait until you get a load of D.C.
Gut Punch Rating: 3
Favorite Quote: "What's a nice girl like you doing in a place like this?"~Nick

The whole world is praying for Nichole's return, and June's glad. If they're praying, that means Gilead doesn't have Nichole. Yet. Meanwhile, June's praying for "Serena to see beyond her heartbreak or that she and Fred get hit by a fucking truck. I'm honestly down for either."

June is on loan to the Waterfords as they head to Washington D.C. for their prayer tour of Gilead. And Aunt Lydia is along for the train ride to hell. Luckily, it seems like an uneventful trip. When they get to D.C., the Washington Monument has been modified to look like a gigantic cross, and handmaids all have on facemasks.

They're on their way to High Commander Winslow's house. High Commander. That must mean he's extra douchey. Winslow is

153

played by a studly Christopher Meloni, who is setting off my gaydar something fierce. I swear he's hitting on Fred.

Winslow and his wife Olivia, have six children of all different ages and race. SIX! Jeez, you think they could spare one for Serena? That would solve all our problems. They also have a Handmaid, Ofgeorge. I guess they're trying for seven.

While everyone is sent to their rooms for the night, Serena mulls over the dossier file the Gilead drones gave her of Nichole's footprints. June is trying to bond with Ofgeorge, but...HER FUCKING LIPS ARE STAPLED SHUT!

What the serious fuck?

The next day, there is a great shot of June standing in front of a winged monument. She looks like a very determined pissed off angel.

"How many of these videos is he going to do?" June asks Serena.

"As many as it takes," Serena replies.

Nick shows up and tells Fred, who is a little unnerved, that Winslow sent him over. It's not only Fred who is in the big guy's good graces. On his way to the front, Nick manages to touch fingers with June.

Fred gets a victory of a sort. The Swiss have agreed to be a neutral party and conduct interviews in hopes that Canada will make a deal. They want to speak to June alone.

"Don't be stupid," Serena warns her, but it doesn't faze June.

The Swiss are maddeningly Swiss and don't seem to care that June is Nichole's mother, that she wants her to stay in Canada. They also seem to know that Fred is not the baby's father, but they don't seem to care about that either. When June offers to get the father, Nick, to roll over on Gilead, they suddenly seem interested.

Back at the Winslows, Fred and George are shooting pool and George is getting a little handsy with Fred. Maybe he's just like that. Maybe. Fred on the other hand doesn't seem too thrilled when their pool game is interrupted by Winslow's daughter's tea party.

However, Serena is enchanted with Fred playing with the stuffed animal. In fact, Serena is enchanted by the Winslows' perfect life. It's everything Gilead should have been for her. Olivia has multiple children (and nannies) and the freedom of being adored by her husband and friends. She's beautiful, happy, and in command of her life. When she mentions that she was a fan of Serena's book, *A Woman's Place*, that cements it in Serena's mind. Serena was a fool for listening to June. D.C. is where she and Fred belong, with June far away in Massachusetts. She is reaffirmed that suffering is for other women, not for her, because they deserve it and she's a commander's wife.

Later that night, Nick sends for June. It's good to be a commander, even in D.C., and they kiss in the frigid Washington air. She tries to convince him to go to the Swiss, but Nick is all like fuck the politicians. They don't give a shit about them. And he's right. June then plays hardball and tells Nick that this is his one chance to act like Nichole's father. Guilted into doing the right thing, Nick agrees to talk with the Swiss.

But everything falls apart the next day. The Swiss don't want to talk with Nick. They believe he can't be trusted. Serena takes great joy in telling June that "Nick was a soldier in the crusade. We wouldn't be here without him. All that time you spent with him and he never mentioned it?"

Bitch.

What the hell Nick?

We get a shot of him walking down a train car all Gestapo like. In fact, all of Washington looks like a Nazi wet dream, with flags flying and an air of supremacy. Alaska is supposed to be the capital of Gilead, but D.C. is looking pretty dystopian headquarters, if you ask me. Say goodbye to Nick. This is the last time we see him. Whether he comes back in Season Four, though, is anyone's guess.

As Aunt Lydia helps June get dressed for the next video extravaganza, she is disturbed by the mouth coverings and answers June's tearful question with, "No, I don't want to see you silenced. When I get tired, I still try to think of the good I can do in God's world. If I can help just one person, one soul, that's enough. I think of you dear."

Yanno, when she's not zapping her with a cattle prod or threatening to send her to the wall. Needless to say, Aunt Lydia still makes June wear the mouthpiece.

June is staring at the ruins of the Lincoln Memorial when Serena approaches her and makes a smart comment about her mouth covering.

"This is nice. The silence."

"You could return the favor," June says, pulling down the mask.

"Let's just stop. You're going to go home. We're staying in D.C. We'll finally be free of each other," Serena says. She must hate that June doesn't let her get away with her sick fantasies of utopia.

"You will never be free of me. You will never be free of me until both of my children are safe." *Atta girl, June.*

"That is my constant prayer for Nichole." Serena reverts back to her kind, butter won't melt in her mouth responses, like a sweet, docile, Gilead wife.

"I trusted you. To let her have the best life possible. To do the right thing."

But that sweet Gilead shit doesn't last long with Serena and she bites back with, "And I trusted you to stay with her."

"I gave her the name of Nichole. I did that to honor you for getting her out. You will not let her go." June is fueled only by hate now towards backbiting Serena.

The fight gets even more vicious when Serena says, "I should have put a ring in your mouth the day we met."

And June blasts back, "I should have let you burn when I had the chance."

I hope those are the last words these two say to each other, because it's perfect.

They join Fred in front of the reflecting pool where hundreds of handmaids are kneeling, lined with the banners of Gilead. Fred has to ask twice, but June slowly sinks to her knees to start the prayers. I wanted her to pull down her mask and have the other handmaids do the same so the world could see what they've done to their mouths. But I doubt it was televised live.

Self-Care Suggestion:

Just when you thought Gilead couldn't get anymore repulsive, they put lip rings on the handmaids to go with the cuffs they staple on their ears. It's so disgusting and demeaning. To try and keep it in perspective, put on your brightest shade of lipstick today and sing loudly along with your favorite song. We have our voices. And for now, our bodies and lips are our own. And you might want to put on a few episodes of *Law and Order: SVU*. Stabler is much nicer to watch than Winslow.

Chapter Thirty: Alice Down the Rabbit Hole

Season Three, Episode Seven: Under His Eye

"I saw you at Loaves and Fishes talking to that Martha. Aunt Lydia told me to watch you. To try and protect you."~Ofmatthew

"What did you say to her?"~June

"I saved you. We saved you. "~Ofmatthew

"You "saved" me? What did you do? What did you do? Do you have any idea what you did? Do you? You fucking bitch! Do you?"~June

Trigger Warnings: Death and blood, hangings
Gut Punch Rating: 3
Favorite Quote: "You killed anybody since you've been out?" – Moira
"No. You?" – Emily
"Nope. So I think we're good." – Moira

The episode starts with a thick red rope and my first thought is, "I wonder whose blood it is?" Then the handmaids walk the line and I start to wonder what fresh hell this new ceremony is. It's just another particicution where, instead of stoning the guilty to death or ripping them apart with their bare hands, they pull the rope and hang the heretics. And it's the fourth one this week.

Janine is upset, June is angry, and Ofmatthew is snippier than usual. "It's cramps," she explains, rubbing her stomach. "This time is difficult." For a minute, June thinks Ofmatthew is going to denounce Gilead because she's just not feeling being pregnant for the fourth time around. But she snaps back to the party line.

157

At Loaves and Fishes, June meets up with Hannah's Martha and tells her that Lawrence can get the three of them (Hannah, June and the Martha) out of Gilead. Reluctantly, the Martha confirms Hannah's school and tells her to ask for a certain guard.

But in the distance, Ofmatthew is watching. This isn't going to end well.

Meanwhile in D.C., Olivia and Serena are gliding through an "unrestored" house. The previous owners were Baptists and their things were left as if they were coming back soon, rather than being strung up on the wall. But Serena doesn't see the things that were smashed in the struggle. She's only enchanted by the nursery.

But where is baby Phoebe, whose name is still on the wall?

Back in Boston, June is desperate to see Hannah. She brings Eleanor her tea and, instead of leaving it at the door, pushes her way in, opening the drapes wide for the sunlight to pour in.

"Do you want to go for a walk?" June asks.

"Joseph wouldn't like it," Eleanor says sadly.

June convinces her to go. This isn't going to end well either. Lawrence is hella protective of his wife and she is so very fragile. On their walk, they meet Naomi Putnam and baby Angela. Eleanor is so happy to see Angela, she keeps repeating, "I'm glad she didn't die" until June gently guides her away.

Back in Canada, Moira and Emily are having coffee and a stab at normality. Moira has to leave to go to a protest and at the last minute Emily decides to join her. At first, Emily is terrified of the crowd, of the anger, until hearing that June wanted her baby back.

"No, she doesn't. She wanted her to be free and to live in Canada. That's why she gave her to me." It's good to see the old Emily back. And she really gives the Canadian minister hell. So much so that they're both taken off to jail.

Moira and Emily bond in the jail cell, helping Emily heal a little more knowing that Moira understands and has been through similar experiences. Knowing that Sylvia is there and supportive too, really helps. Especially after Emily had been interrogated by the Swiss that morning. Sylvia had yelled at the Swiss investigator and told Emily that she didn't care what she had to do to survive in Gilead.

Meanwhile, June and Eleanor pause at a bridge when Eleanor shows signs of breaking down. June comes clean then, telling her that she really just wants to see Hannah. She apologizes and says she'll take her home, but Eleanor rallies and decides that they'll go to Hannah's school.

Commander Lawrence's name opens up a lot of doors, allowing Eleanor admission, but not June. June follows the wall to find the playground to see Hannah, but it's completely walled up with razor wire on the top. She can hear Hannah laughing and playing, but she can't see her.

June sinks to her knees in agony, and when Eleanor has another breakdown, a guard drags June away. Back at the house, Lawrence escorts his wife upstairs. She's distraught and sick. He takes care of her and tucks her into bed.

I am literally shaking for June. We've seen him explode on her when she asked about her health. What is he going to do now when she actually caused Eleanor to suffer?

June gets ahead of him though, by saying she never wanted to hurt her and that "you should have seen her. She came alive."

And it's enough to stave off whatever punishment Lawrence had in mind.

Back in D.C., Fred and Serena are at a swanky Gilead dinner tango to thunderous applause. The wives are eyeballing handsome young guards and Serena isn't sure how to react at that.

In Boston, there are more hangings and up on the scaffold is Hannah's Martha. The MacKenzies are gone too, without a trace. June refuses to pick up the rope, but Aunt Lydia is waiting for this. "Ofjoseph, no one can escape their sacred duty."

Ofmatthew is looking very smug. No doubt in my mind that she ratted them all out.

Hannah is gone. There will be no rescue out of Gilead now.

"Disperse," Aunt Lydia says after the heretics are dead.

June is the last to go, but she pushes her way up to Ofmatthew and confronts her. The other handmaids move in to block the view of them, so that the guards and the Aunts can't see June choking Ofmatthew. Ofmatthew, on the direction of Aunt Lydia, had been spying on her. And she truly believes she was saving June.

They have to pull June off her as Fiona Apple sings "Every Single Night."

Self-Care Suggestion:

Hannah has disappeared as effectively as Nichole, only June doesn't have the power to go on television and demand her return. Luke should be doing that, but he's not. And I'm still going back and forth on the mystery that is Nick. What's his end game? I believe that he was instrumental in setting up Gilead, but I also believe that like Lawrence, he believes that Gilead took a wrong turn at Albuquerque somewhere. But he's on the front, a commander in his own right. Perhaps he can get a line on Hannah. I can't believe that all is lost. But I'm afraid that Hannah is lost in the system.

Consider making a donation to an anti-child trafficking organization or offer to volunteer to help a children's organization or a child in need. We can make a difference and every little bit counts.

Chapter Thirty-One: No More Fucks to Give

Season Three, Episode Eight: Unfit

"You act like you care about your wife.... I know you don't give a shit about the rest of us. But you do realize that this world that you built here is destroying her. And that with one phone call, you could have her out. But you're keeping her hostage. You're not protecting her. You're killing her."~June

"I'll bet that felt good."~Commander Lawrence

Trigger Warnings: June might be lost to us, beatings, blood, murder
Gut Punch Rating: 3
Haunting Quote: "There's an acquired taste to seeing others in pain. Like that smoky Scotch Luke got as a gift once. I grew to like that."~June

The handmaids are at another birth ceremony now. While Ofandy is struggling, June is hanging back watching the spectacle and visibly seething. The other handmaids are doing their damnedest to make Ofmatthew's life difficult. From poking her, to spitting in her water, to blocking her from talking to June, Ofmatthew is persona non grata in their world. So much so that Aunt Lydia orders June to tell her friends to knock it off.

June basically says, "Make me."

And Aunt Lydia takes up the challenge. As June points out, Aunt Lydia can't rip out her eye or cut out her tongue, because Gilead may need her on camera at some point. But Aunt Lydia is not above putting her in the shame circle. At first June's like, "Yes, it's my fault. I'm fucking responsible for Frances being hung." Frances was Hannah's Martha.

161

But it's not going to be that easy. Aunt Lydia knows how to twist the knife and she tells her that not only did Agnes/Hannah lose someone who loved and cared for her, but Hannah's world is now "emptier and colder than it ever was." I don't buy that, as Mrs. MacKenzie seemed like a decent sort. But June believes it.

"You wicked, selfish fool," Aunt Lydia snarls.

June rallies though. She knows how to push Aunt Lydia's buttons too. She testifies that Ofmatthew doesn't want her baby, which is also not technically true. As Ofmatthew said, it was only for a moment, but that's enough to ignite Aunt Lydia and Ofmatthew is put in the shame circle where the Handmaids let her have it.

"Sinner!"

"Crybaby!"

I'm sure that worked out well for Aunt Lydia because it gave them a way to vent their outrage on Ofmatthew. June enjoys Ofmatthew's torment, though, and that's not like her.

When Ofandy's baby finally does come however, it's stillborn, and when the other Handmaids go to hug Ofandy, June fades into the background to look at the dead child. Instead of sorrow, she feels relief and happiness that this baby will be spared a life in Gilead. After all, a female in Gilead is either a Martha, a Jezebel, a Handmaid, or a Wife. Unless they're shipped off to the colonies for being an Unwoman.

We get a flashback to Aunt Lydia's life pre-Gilead. She was an ultra-religious spinster who loved children—and get this—was a fucking kindergarten teacher. Although, there is a mention that she was a family attorney at one point as well, but she couldn't help all the children that she wanted. I'm not too happy with Aunt Lydia's backstory and I don't believe it.

She starts off as a good Christian woman who looks after a single mother and her son, who is in her class. She was kind to them and they became like her family. So much so that the mother encourages her to go out and date. She even buys her make-up and does her face so that Lydia can go out on New Year's Eve with the principal of their school. It's a fun date that has Lydia drinking and doing karaoke, and then back to her house for some necking.

Only, Lydia gets a little aggressive and her date doesn't say "Hell no." He just says slow down. Well, Lydia is mortified over her sinful urges and that turns her into ultra bitch. In the next scene, she's calling child services on the mom and the boy is taken away. All because Lydia wanted the "D."

No. I'm not buying it.

I get that she was sexually repressed and a religious fanatic to begin with, and it was no secret that she thought the boy's mother was unfit. But I don't buy that she would use that as reason to destroy a family she had grown close to. And in doing so, alienated the principal even more. He didn't say no. He had just said, not yet.

It makes her no better than the commander rapists, and that's a waste of a good villain. The catalyst of her transformation should not be because she didn't get dicked. Pisses me off. I'm glad that by the time I saw this episode, I had read Margaret Atwood's sequel to *The Handmaid's Tale*. *The Testaments* goes into much more detail about what turned Lydia into an Aunt and it's much more believable.

No spoilers though! Go read the book. It's amazing.

The other thing that pissed me off in Aunt Lydia's backstory though? She was divorced. Well, not according to Gilead's law. Where is her husband then, I wonder?

Back in Gilead we see the Aunts choosing where to place the handmaids, while drinking tea and spinning a large wooden Lazy Susan filled with dossiers. Lydia has had enough of June's shit. She's going to reassign her away from the Lawrences and goes to Loaves and Fishes to tell her.

But Ofmatthew is watching them. And she's a nervous wreck. In addition to being pregnant, and having to go through emotional and light physical abuse from her other handmaids, she can't help but wonder what June and Aunt Lydia are talking about.

June sees this and wants her to suffer, so she turns her head just so and smirks. Janine picks the wrong time to comfort Ofmatthew, who turns on her and beats her with a canned jar.

"Natalie, no!" Aunt Lydia screams. It's strange how she knows all their names and only uses them when she's trying to reach them after they've spiraled down into madness.

When the guardian tries to break it up, Ofmattew smashes a glass jar over their head, cutting his throat. She then grabs his gun and turns it on everyone as they run for cover. Everyone except for Aunt Lydia and June.

163

June smirks again, but glances at Aunt Lydia. You can tell she doesn't care if she dies or not.

Ofmatthew though, swings the gun toward Aunt Lydia, but before she can get off a shot, is shot herself. June doesn't seem to care. In fact, she seems to enjoy what has just happened. Losing Hannah has broken her and Ofmatthew paid for her treachery with her death.

The guardians drag out Ofmatthew's body, as we get a close up of June's blank face while Doris Day sings, "Que Sera Sera."

Self-Care Suggestion:

The red on the white snow, the callous look in June's eyes, her smile as she eagerly awaits the bullet, this isn't our heroine. This isn't the June we've been on this journey with since Episode One. But events can spiral out of control and things happen that make us feel powerless and afraid. Some of us lash out. Some of us retreat into ourselves. If you're hurting or you're numb—even if it has nothing to do with this binge watch—reach out to someone. Talk with a therapist or a professional, or if you're not ready to do that, with a trusted friend. You are loved and you are worth it. You are not alone.

Chapter Thirty-Two: Do You Know What That's Worth?

Season Three, Episode Nine: Heroic

"I'm sorry I was such a shit to you. I got lost I think. Not that that's a good excuse, but I don't really have another reason. They just take everything from you, you know? They really do."~June

Trigger Warnings: descent into madness, suicide attempt, murder attempt, blood, surgery, graphic evidence that in Gilead a woman's only worth is her uterus.
Gut Punch Rating: 5

Fuck, this is a heavy episode.

Well, it seems like Ofmatthew, or Natalie as we found out last episode, is only mostly dead. Belinda Carlisle sings, "Heaven is a Place on Earth" while Natalie is hooked up to machines. June is singing it in her head over and over again. "Don't you hear it?" she asks us as the monitors blip and beep. "You will."

June remarks that the doctors don't give Natalie anything to hurt the baby, but they also aren't doing anything to save her. Natalie's lost too much blood. She's brain dead and I think June is right behind her in losing her mind. Natalie "is just a vessel. The baby is all that matters now. I guess it was all that ever mattered," June says in her hazy thoughts that drift in and out of sanity.

June has been kneeling at Natalie's hospital bedside, stark red on the white floor for 32 days now. She'll be there until there is either a baby or Natalie is dead. "This is your walking partner," Aunt Lydia says. "Where else would you be?"

Half in and out of consciousness, June's mind is wandering and

165

rambling. She sees the wives come to pray for the baby. "It smells like baby powder," June thinks without emotion. "Like Serena Joy when she held me down during the ceremony."

The pink clad daughters parade by the window as June struggles to comprehend if she really sees them or not. Then she realizes they're there for their checkups to make sure once they can handle childbirth, they can be married off.

At night, June tries to stand. Her knees are bruised and bloody, and her legs don't hold her on the first attempt. She goes to Natalie's bedside and grips the breathing tube, to stop her oxygen, but the lights come on and bring the doctors.

"Please God. Let them die," June prays, referring to Natalie and the baby, but later she considers killing the doctors.

The next day, June asks Aunt Lydia if she could go home, but Aunt Lydia refuses. In her mind, it's the least June could do after the way she and the other handmaids treated Natalie. June is suffering, both mentally and physically, and asks to be sent home because she doesn't feel well. Aunt Lydia tells June to keep praying, that the Lord doesn't give them more than they can bear.

But after she leaves, June who is sleep deprived and delusional, considers the sharp box where the needles were disposed. She reaches in and is stabbed, but she keeps going until she finds the scalpel the doctors used. But just before she's about to slit Natalie's throat, Janine comes in.

Her eye was infected after not healing right from the wounds she got when Natalie beat her, and that's why she's in the hospital. Janine is blaming herself for Natalie's condition because she hasn't been praying for her. She asks June if she thinks Natalie can hear her. June says she doesn't know. Janine takes a deep breath and tells Natalie that she forgives her and wants her to get better.

"She can't get better," June says.

Janine shrugs and said, "We can wish for it anyway." Which really sums up Janine's new attitude in Gilead.

But then, June shows her the scalpel and tells her that they could basically put Natalie out of her misery.

"No," Janine says. When Janine is the sane one in the conversation, you know you're in trouble. If June kills Natalie, she's going to be executed.

"It's the kind thing to do," June claims. She hates that Natalie is suffering, but she's also dancing with madness and I'm not sure her motives are a hundred percent altruistic.

"Kill her?" Janine begs her not to.

June smiles and says, "Okay."

Janine believes her, but asks for the scalpel. Not so dumb after all.

June refuses.

"When did you get to be so selfish? Everything is about you now," she mutters when June won't give it up.

June tells her to get the fuck out. The next day, June is trying to decide who to kill. Should it be the commander, the wife or the doctor? She knows she's only getting one kill, one shot. Then, Serena walks in.

Bingo! We have a winner. When everybody goes to leave, June calls Serena over. "Come closer. It's a secret."

Serena does, but when June staggers to her feet, she can see that June isn't doing well at all. In the next instant, she slashes Serena with the scalpel. But Serena is stronger and manages to get the scalpel away from her, before cutting her back.

"Please end it," June says, lying on the floor.

"You were supposed to be one of the strong ones," Serena says in disgust. She leaves, but sends the doctor in for June's wounds. He disposes of the scalpel and tells her she needs stitches. June tells him he shouldn't bother healing her that they're just going to take her away for attacking Serena.

He replies that he took an oath to heal patients, and that Serena didn't seem too keen on informing the guardians about the attack. June accuses the doctor of torturing Natalie, but he tells her the baby is the patient. And June says, "Bullshit. My mother was a doctor. She took care of her patients, the mothers, first."

"That was a long time ago. I hope she got out."

June admits that she doesn't know. She saw her picture in a slide show of the colonies and it's been five years, so chances are that no, Dr. Holly Maddox isn't alive anymore. But she tells the doctor about her anyway.

The doctor recognizes the name. "Dr. Maddox. She was scary. Now I know why you took a swipe at Mrs. Waterford."

He talks to June about her suicide wish—which is what killing anyone in the hospital would be. And how it was because June's brain was atrophying from being in the room praying on her knees for months on end.

June said it started when she lost her daughters.

"I honor the handmaid by keeping her child alive," the doctor said. "How will you honor your daughters?"

It gives June something to think about, and a life line to grab onto and drag herself back to sanity.

Meanwhile, Natalie's baby has to be cut out of her, because her body is failing and she is slowly dying. Both the seizures and being hooked up on the machines have taken their toll on her body. But the boy is alive. Natalie is allowed to die and it is only a matter of time. June is allowed to go home.

As she staggers down the hallway on knees that are no doubt hurting and sore, one of the pink clad girls offers to carry June's suitcase. Her name is Rose and she is here because they wanted to make sure she was ready to have a baby. She's all of 14.

"Is that what you want?" June asks and Rose pauses before saying, "Of course."

If Gilead has only been around for five years, this girl was nine when she was taken from her family. She remembers a pre-Gilead world. All the girls this age do.

While June enjoys the sweet air of freedom, more pink clad girls are escorted inside for their pregnancy readiness checkups. When Aunt Lydia arrives to take her home, June decides that she wants to stay with Natalie until the end.

"Go with grace," Aunt Lydia said, proud of her.

"I'll try," June says.

Aunt Lydia comes to the hospital to visit Janine. Her procedure was a success, but she is fretting about her lack of an eye and how bad the wound looks. Aunt Lydia has brought Janine a red eyepatch, and Janine cries and smiles at the kindness. "I look like a pirate," she says.

"Indeed." Aunt Lydia laughs.

I don't get it. Why the little kindnesses? Why the red eye patch when we know Aunt Lydia hates vanity. I suppose it's her way of apologizing for beating the shit out of her at the Putnam's christening. Janine has been everybody's punching bag.

168

Sitting at Natalie's bedside, June apologizes to Natalie and makes a vow. "Your son is beautiful. He doesn't deserve to grow up in this place. He deserves to be free. They all deserve to be free. So, Natalie, I'm going to get them out. I'm going to get out as many children as I can. I don't know how, but I swear to you. I'm going to get them out. Because Gilead should know how this feels. It's their turn to hurt."

Well, this is certainly going to be interesting.

Self-Care Suggestion:

It's nice to see June all fired up and in her right mind again. She's come to terms that Hannah is lost to her and seems to have set her sight on a new goal. Taking down Gilead and hurting them like they've hurt others. She's living for revenge now and even more I wonder if June can survive this new page in her book. I think she's going to burn out and there will be nothing left of the pre-Gilead June Osborne.

This episode felt claustrophobic to me. All that white, the white walls of the hospital room. If you felt the same, go outside and take deep breaths. Take your phone and do a yoga class in the sun. Or if it's raining, take an umbrella and listen to a meditation tape.

And as much as I love the GoGos and Belinda Carlyle, don't play "Heaven is a Place on Earth."

Chapter Thirty-Three: What Has This Season Has Been Lacking?

Season Three, Episode Ten: Witness

"You just treat it like a job. Try to detach yourself. See from the outside. You're not you, I'm not me. This is a transaction and then it's over." You just treat it like a job. Try to detach yourself. See from the outside. You're not you, I'm not me. This is a transaction and then it's over."~June

Trigger Warnings: Rape
Gut Punch Rating: 4

June staggers back to the Lawrence household, walking as fast as her ruined knees will let her. I'm not sure why she's going back when Aunt Lydia had decided to pull her out and give her to another family. I suppose with Natalie's death and June's apparent change of heart, Aunt Lydia is going to give her one more chance.

Back at the Lawrence's, the household has changed. Commander Waterford has put orders in to standardize all the households to boring. All of Lawrence's books and artwork are gone.

"I believe my time of prayer has led me to see my true purpose," June says to Aunt Lydia before she leaves.

"Oh, you are a good girl," Aunt Lydia coos, believing that June has finally, FINALLY, seen the light.

Aunt Lydia's instincts are good, but she's sometimes blind to what her charges are really capable of—especially when their backs are to the wall, which Aunt Lydia excels at pushing them to. For some reason, she's got a soft spot for June and I don't know why. She should know by now that June is nothing but trouble.

171

Sienna and Beth are still Marthas in the household, and Beth welcomes June by pointing to a basket of scones. "Scones mean no," she says. Eleanor is no longer allowed her bipolar medication. When they can't acquire black market medications or any other request, the Marthas send scones. How awesome is it that the resistance/black market/Mayday uses baked goods to communicate?

June tells Beth that she wants to rescue children out of Gilead, and Beth tells her that she's going to get herself killed.

Meanwhile, Eleanor is having a breakdown upstairs, screaming and crying.

"She throws things now," Beth tells June.

"Welcome home," Lawrence says dryly, before going into his office, stuffed with his forbidden books.

June suggests he leave Gilead with his wife. "Get a truck. Get her out. Get her the help that she needs."

Lawrence is considering it.

"She can't take much more of this," June warns.

"What do you know about how much someone can take?" Lawrence scoffs.

"Everything," June whispers.

Lawrence is listening.

"He's scared. Fear can be a great motivator," June thinks, smiling as she leaves his office. If she can't manipulate him through sex, she can use his love for his wife to get him to do what she wants.

Striding into Loaves and Fishes, June notices that the other handmaids give her a wide berth. "Another walking partner dead," she thinks. "They must think I'm cursed or a terrorist. I'm not. Not yet."

Boston has definitely changed while June was inside the hospital. There are armed guards in every corner now. She tries to talk to Alma.

"I can't help," she mutters. "They're watching everything we do, and you're really conspicuous."

June ignores that and asks how many handmaids still have children in the district. She's going to get them out of Gilead.

Alma tells her she's going on the wall just for thinking that. "Are you okay?

"No, I'm not fucking okay."

They're called to assembly and all the handmaids are pressed together in an outside amphitheater for their special guest. Fred is their important visitor? Oh, it's Winslow. This can't be good.

Fred makes a beeline for June. "You're looking well," he says to her, breaking all sorts of protocol.

"Blessed be the fruit," June responds, not wanting to get in trouble.

"It's much warmer in D.C. I might be able to obtain a transfer for you," he oozes.

"Your wife is here." June points out Serena who isn't looking too happy. Fred hasn't been in Boston two seconds before getting up to his old tricks.

Winslow faces off against Aunt Lydia, bitching that Janine's eyepatch isn't regulation. But Aunt Lydia is unconcerned. She tells him it was approved and she stands by it. She asks about the ring for their mouths.

It's going to be voluntary. At first.

Oh wonderful. Isn't that nice? Who the heck is going to volunteer to have their lips sewn shut?

Serena and June size each other up with a few snarky lines, before Winslow descends upon them. It makes you wonder what Fred has said about June to him.

"How does Joseph treat you?" Winslow asks.

Stunned, June replies honestly. "He treats me with respect."

Respect?

You can almost hear Fred groan, and Serena shoots her a dirty look.

"I'm grateful to be of service," June quickly finishes.

After the ceremony, June hobbles back to the Lawrences and gets caught rifling through his files by Eleanor. She comes clean and says she's looking for her friends' children. Eleanor said the Red Center dossier files are in the basement.

That was easy.

"Let's go. I don't have all day," Eleanor says.

Due to the time on her knees, June can no longer walk without staggering, but nothing is going to stop her from getting down those stairs. Eleanor finds her the files, of which June reads her own, but there isn't anything new about Agnes' whereabouts. While they're

173

down there, June asks Eleanor if she's ever thought about leaving Gilead.

"And get mood enhancing drugs instead of herbal tea?" Eleanor is a pip when she's lucid. I hate that Gilead has turned her into what Joseph calls "fragile." And as much as she loathes what he's done, she does still love him. "Joseph is a war criminal. He can't cross the border. He'll be jailed or killed, and he'd deserve it."

Back at the Waterfords, however, evil doesn't rest. Winslow is grinning at Serena, who's been asking too many smart questions. Fred brings up that Commander Lawrence is hanging on to the old ways. "His influence does more harm than good. He's had four Handmaids and not one has produced. We need to set an example," Fred says on a power-hungry trip.

Yeah, like this isn't some twisted way to see June again. Or to try and maneuver her back into his household. I don't get the obsession. Maybe it's a revenge thing for making him look like an incompetent ass and turning his wife against him, or some bullshit in his mind like that.

"Challenging Lawrence is delicate," Winslow says. They were old buddies, but if he actually *respects* his Handmaid...

Serena butts in and defends Lawrence—not for any reason other than she wants Fred and June far away from each other.

Well, that settles the matter for Winslow. If Serena is on Lawrence's side, then something's off. "If he's unfit to lead his household, he's unfit to lead Gilead."

During all this, June is still in the basement going through the records. "Five years since we've had our children taken away from us. They were seven. Now they're 12. We've missed everything," she laments. Poor Janine's son, Caleb, died in a car accident. That would push Janine over the thin line of sanity.

Beth interrupts, coming to get June. They have guests. It's ceremony night. June kneels on the pillow wondering what the heck is going on, but Beth and Sienna don't even know what to do. There has never been a ceremony in this house.

June remembers in the early days of Gilead, when people were hesitant to perform the ceremony, a group of commanders would bear witness to the event to make sure it happened. This is what is happening here.

Serena enters with Eleanor, who looks haunted. "What a lovely room," Serena says.

She is such a bitch.

"I pray nothing will impede God's will tonight," Serena warns, glaring at June.

Lawrence knocks and is offered to come into the parlor, as Serena reminds Eleanor with a nudge of the wife's part. Fred and Winslow follow Lawrence into the room, apologizing for barging in to bear witness. Yeah, he's real fucking sorry. Aunt Lydia is there too. Were they selling tickets? I bet they'd make a killing on concessions. Beth is an awesome cook after all. I wonder if there are any nope scones left?

"Are you going to sit on the bed with us too? Because that will definitely make things more interesting," Lawrence says, but he's too nervous to deliver it with the usual bite in his voice.

Lawrence reads from the Bible while I just want to punch Fred in his smiling, swarmy face. And then it's time to go up the stairs for the ceremony. The spook squad stays downstairs for the world's most awkward coffee klatch.

June makes her way up the stairs, her knees still giving her trouble, and once the bedroom door is closed, it's an awkward scene.

"We'll sit here quietly for 20 minutes and then we'll go down. We can play canasta," Lawrence said, just barely holding on to his panic.

June delivers the bad news. "The doctor will check me to make sure the ceremony happens."

"You swore we would never have to do this," Eleanor said, losing her shit so loud that everyone is afraid of being outed and taken away.

"You made this world. Didn't you think it would come for you?" June says, not believing the bullshit in front of her. From Serena on down to Eleanor, these wives are just as much to blame as their husbands. They accepted it. They allowed it.

That being said, when Eleanor is faced with it and can't look away, she's willing to take responsibility for it. "We won't. You'll be fine. It's our sin." She's willing to hang with her husband so that they won't have to rape June.

Now it's Lawrence's turn to deliver the bad news. "Handmaids are required to report deviants."

175

"Martha's too," June adds.

Eleanor shatters when she realizes that her husband will have to rape June, or everyone in the household will be executed. But, she has the luxury to leave the room while it happens. It's destroyed every last bit of normalcy she had been clinging to.

Lawrence reminds me of Nick when he had to deflower Eden. He's doesn't want to do it, but it's his death if he doesn't.

"It's easier if you close your eyes," June tells him, ironically comforting her soon-to-be-rapist. Talk about the emotional labor of a woman's work.

Thankfully, they don't show the rape. But they do show Eleanor and her despair, as well as June steeling herself to be raped yet again.

Back downstairs, it's a solemn and quiet event. Fred pours the tea. Lawrence comes down the stairs without a word and goes into his office. Aunt Lydia and Serena come up to check on Eleanor, who apologizes that it's been so long since they've had dinner. But Eleanor is holding on by a thread. Serena offers her comfort, probably thinking that she's worried her husband likes banging the handmaid better than he likes having sex with her.

Aunt Lydia waits with a stone-faced June, who is poised there for her gyno exam. The doctor gives her the thumbs up. Apparently, Lawrence's dick got hard and he pumped her full of semen.

Downstairs, Aunt Lydia cheerfully pronounces a successful ceremony. Fred looks like he's swallowed a lemon. "Praised be."

"How are you?" Fred asks, sidling up to June.

"At least it wasn't you," June tells him, before walking away.

Serena watches in disgust. She can't figure out what Fred's obsession with June is.

Later, June finds Lawrence in the kitchen and asks about Eleanor.

"She's very quiet." He hands June birth control pills.

"The punishment for contraception is being torn apart by dogs," June informs him.

"I'll get you a truck," he said. "You get my wife out safely."

It's a small victory. But at least it's something.

"You can get out too," June tells him. "You just have to bring them something valuable. Kids. The stolen children of Gilead."

"I'd be a hero," he snorts. But it's not a no. He's taking her seriously.

At Loaves and Fishes, Alma practically runs away from June, until she says the magic words.

"Dillon's new name is Joshua. And he's blond."

Alma reels from hearing her son's name for the first time in five years. "His daddy's blond," she whispers, stunned.

"How long are we going to let Gilead keep him?" June persuades. "I have a truck that can fit 10."

"We can't do this alone," Alma says. She's on board now too.

"I can help," Janine volunteers.

Everyone jumps, not expecting her to be listening and lucid.

"I'm brave," she says. Then, since she knows June has been looking at all their files, she asks June about her own son, Caleb. June lies and said his family moved to California, that they live on the beach.

"His mom is super nice."

Janine is devastated, but she smiles thinking that her baby has a great life. Oh Janine. I'm so glad June got her kindness back.

Back at the Waterford's Serena approaches Fred and you can tell by the look in his eyes that he knows she's about to rip him a new asshole.

"I know last night was difficult. Thank you for your resilience."

F-f-f-f-uck you.

"We have to be a united front," she says.

And you too.

But then she accuses him of concentrating too much on his career and not enough on getting Nichole back. Frankly, I think he's forgotten Nichole is a baby. She's just a way to promote himself and keep June in his life.

Luckily, Serena has a plan. She tells Fred that she met someone in Canada—an American who is willing to help them as long as they give him some information.

Could this be Mark of the coconuts and Hawaii offer?

What is Serena up to?

It can't be good.

Back at the Lawrence household, Beth is staring in disbelief around her kitchen. "Whatever you asked?" she says to June. "Muffins mean yes." The kitchen is full of muffin baskets.

Fifty two Marthas said they would deliver children to them so they can escape Gilead.

"We're going to need a bigger boat," June says.

177

Self-Care Suggestion:
Make muffins to celebrate all those children that are hopefully going to get out of Gilead. And the next time someone asks you to do something you don't want to, bake some scones.

Chapter Thirty-Four: Karma is Only a Bitch if You Are

Season Three, Episode Eleven: Liars

Fifty-two. Marthas and handmaids are offering to help me get fifty-two kids out. Fifty-two kids, and ten seats. How does that math work? Moira would tell me I need to keep my fucking shit together." ~June

Trigger Warnings: death, attempted rape, attempted murder
Gut Punch Rating: 3
Favorite Quote: "You jumped onto a train that was already moving and you think you're Che fucking Guevara."—Mayday Martha

Payoff baby. Three seasons and finally, a bunch of commanders get what's coming to them. This is a glorious episode. Grab the popcorn and settle in.

The episode opens up with June trying to figure out a way to get 52 kids out of Gilead, but is distracted by a group of raised voices from the other room. Going out to investigate, June finds Eleanor holding a shaky gun to her kneeling husband's forehead. She's going to blow his head off for raping June. Lawrence has lost complete control of his household and it's up to June to talk her down.

"I know you want to kill him. I want to kill him too."

Not pulling any punches, June remarks that Eleanor is as much to blame as Lawrence for Gilead's creation.

Eleanor's determined to do something about it now, but June manages to convince her that in order to do a greater good, she needs Lawrence alive. And Eleanor desperately wants to believe they can make difference, so she gives up the gun.

Later on, June and Lawrence share a glass of whiskey together on the couch. When she tells him about her plan to get the kids out,

179

he almost falls off the chair. Like everyone else, he tells her that she is insane—especially when she confirms that she's not leaving with them.

"Mental health was never part of the equation. Maternal love. We overlooked that one too." That's Lawrence's way to make a dry statement underplaying the obvious.

The scene shifts as the Waterfords are going on a road trip. Rita sees them off, expressing concern whether this is the best thing for Nichole. Serena uncharacteristically breaks down in tears and tells Rita, "May the Lord bless you and keep you."

Meanwhile, June has a visit from the Martha Mafia. These are a bunch of tough bitches who don't like that June is muscling in on their action. Beth vouches for her and June agrees not to interfere with their machinations, but they tell her she is on her own. They won't help her if she fails.

Back in the car on the open road, Fred is confident that Serena has pulled the wool over Mark Truello's eyes. They pat each other on the back at how the land has recovered under Gilead's rule. Fred turns off Oprah, and Radio Free America, and offers Serena a chance to drive the sweet little convertible. After demurring, Serena gets behind the wheel, because there is no one around to see.

I find it funny that Fred has taken June's advice and let Serena have a little bit of power behind the scenes. Her grin is wide and excited while she lead foots it down the road, listening to Chubby Checker's "Let's Twist Again."

Back in the Lawrence house, the Commander has gathered up his wife and rabbited. This means that the rescue is off. And that he's making a run for the border on his own. I guess if Fred and Serena can leave to make deals with Americans, so can Joseph and Eleanor. Unfortunately, that leaves Sienna, Beth and June in a shitload of trouble. Not to mention those 52 children that June promised to get out of Gilead.

June comes up with the idea to put the kids on Billy's plane, the one that the Martha's had scheduled and didn't want June's plans to fuck up. She points out that after the plane is empty, they could just load the kids back on it. It solves the problem on how to fit 52 children in a truck with only 10 spaces.

Serena and Fred stay for a night at a large Econofamily's home and have a heart to heart, wondering how different their life would be in Gilead.

"How could you have taken that from me?" Serena asks, when they talked about how happy she had been in their old apartment.

"I didn't know how much it would cost you." Fred almost sounds sincere.

They share a moment when they realize that they both wanted children more than they wanted each other, but that there was still a lot of love between them. Fred even considers retiring from being a Commander to watch "his" daughter grow up. I'm not sure I believe him.

I think he's running another game.

In Boston, Lawrence comes sneaking back into the house. June is sitting at his desk and asks what's he doing back.

"I had an attack of conscience."

"Bullshit."

Bullshit indeed. It seems Commander Lawrence has lost considerable power in Gilead. Fred and Winslow have been busy, and Lawrence's oddities are no longer tolerated in Gilead. Every day he's closer to the wall. He can't even get past the checkpoints anymore. He and Eleanor are stuck. Lawrence knows that it's only a matter of time and offers to keep her out of the colonies, and Jezebels, and find her a kind Commander before he goes.

What a mensch.

But June has other ideas. She makes him drive her to Jezebels so she can talk to the bartender, Billy, who has the Marthas' plane coming in to deliver contraband. The same jet that June is determined to get the 52 children on. And so June returns to Jezebels in a hot little black number and ruby red lipstick. Where the crap did Commander Lawrence get a dress like that? Was it Eleanor's?

At the bar, June bribes Billy with the Picassos and other famous paintings that Lawrence raided from all the museums. He's greedy enough to go for it, but tells her maybe. Triumphant, June is about to leave. But you know it can't be that easy. Guess who's in the bar too? And who happens to recognize her?

Winslow.

After questioning her as to Joseph's whereabouts, June says he's in the car. "He likes me to have fun and then report back to him," she says. That's all Winslow needs to hear before taking June upstairs. She's prepared to let herself be raped again. "I've done this before," she tries to reason with herself. "Treat it like a job."

But something snaps and she lashes out at him. They fight. Winslow is not prepared for this, and when June grabs his pen and stabs him over and over again with it, she gets the upper hand. It's enough for her to snatch up a heavy statue and beat him over the head with it.

That fucker's last words were a plea to June about "his children." Ker-ist, hit him once for me, June. What a dick.

I'm yelling at her to get out, but she's in shock. She sinks to the hotel floor until she's found by one of the women she had helped save from Chicago. She staggers through the halls, bruised and bloody, but no one looks twice at her. Not even a passing Commander and his date for the night. She limps to Lawrence's car, shoeless but determined.

"Drive," she orders a shocked Lawrence.

Back on the Canadian/Gilead border, Fred and Serena wait impatiently for Truello to appear. It is the same American who's been trying to turn Serena. Fred has a moment of trepidation, but Serena convinces him that Mark can be trusted. They follow him "just a few miles" up a twisty isolated road.

I start to feel a little excited. Did Serena play Fred? Is Mark going to backstab both of them? Fred is usually too smart for this and should know what's going on. This reeks of a set up. And sure enough, as soon as they park, the Waterfords are taken into custody and arrested for war crimes. Agent Truello reads them their rights.

Fred is freaking out and demanding that Serena has done nothing wrong.

Personally, I wanted to see the American agents bounce the Waterfords' heads off the car roof a few times, before shoving them into the car. But it was still glorious to hear Mark read the laundry list of crimes they're going to hang on the Waterfords.

And with the Jezebel Martha's getting rid of the evidence and burning Commander Winslow's body, that's two commanders and one bitch wife that Gilead will never see again.

Hasta la vista, motherfuckers!

Back in Boston, Lawrence gives June a loaded pistol.

"They'll be coming for us," he warns her.

June nods, but the sun is shining on her back and lighting up the screen. She's not going down without a fight. She's got children to save. Aunt Lydia would be proud of her dedication to the children—if it wasn't going to pull Gilead inside out.

Self-Care Suggestion:

Oh it's time to celebrate. Break out the good stuff. Champagne, wine, chocolates, whatever you've been saving for a special occasion. I'm just sorry no one spit on the Waterfords when they shoved them in the car.

Chapter Thirty-Five: Oh What a Tangled Web We Weave

Season Three, Episode Twelve: Sacrifice

"Well, you're off the hook, or off the wall, I should say... Cheer up. Fred and Serena are toast and you just got away with murder. All in all, not a bad morning."~Lawrence

Trigger Warnings: assisted suicide, gun violence, madness, funeral
Gut Punch Rating: 3
Favorite Quote: "I pity the child that has you as her mother."—Fred
"I will pray for you, Fred,"—Serena

June hears the van pull up to the house and knows that they're coming for her. She hears boots on the stairs, and when the door opens, she's ready with the pistol. Except it's only Eleanor, who tells her to leave the gun and come downstairs. Beth is going to need her help making coffee and sandwiches for their guests.

Is this one of Eleanor's delusions?

Yet, there hasn't been any gunfire, even though the place is crawling with guardians with assault rifles. Lawrence is meeting with Commanders Putnam and Matthew—Natalie's baby daddy who's cranky because he was up all night with his preemie.

"Sienna busy, is she?" Lawrence says, knowing exactly why June is in the room serving coffee. And yes, muffins.

"Yes sir," June says brightly, which I can only hope gets right under his skin.

Once the Commanders leave, Lawrence tells June that they think Winslow was taken by the Americans. The Waterfords have gone rogue and were ambushed, now facing trial as war criminals in Toronto. June cries and laughs. Everything is going swimmingly.

185

Which usually means something really shitty is going to happen. And not to Fred and Serena, who I'm hoping get the handmaid special in prison.

The plan is to get the kids to the Lawrence household after dark, where trucks will take them to the plane. They're due in just one week. June and Rita have a moment in Loaves and Fishes gleefully picturing Fred and Serena in orange jumpsuits.

"Serena's only nice when she's up to something," June says, when Rita mentions Serena's goodbye.

Hmmm, that's foreshadowing.

Sure enough, Serena made a deal to see Nichole in exchange for giving up Fred.

"My daughter needs me," Serena said, sobbing. I'm surprised Fred didn't try to kill her. On the one hand, I'm thrilled to see Fred betrayed and in prison, but on the other hand I don't think Serena should get off so easily.

Back in the Lawrence residence, Eleanor isn't doing so well. Naomi Putman and Olivia Winslow are there praying for George's return. Yeah, keep praying. Mrs. Winslow is upset that, as a lone woman, they won't let her have the six children.

Aw.

Should have thought of that when you gave up your law degree to fuck over other women and create a shit country like Gilead. Enjoy bitch. I hope they send you to the colonies. If not, you'll make a good Martha. I wonder, what does happen to widows in Gilead? I can't imagine another commander would marry them, when there are younger child brides that are fertile to be had.

"We can take the children with us," Eleanor says, almost blowing it. "We can fit them here."

"Mi casa, es su casa," Lawrence says, covering for her, and luckily they're used to Eleanor being a little odd, so it passes over the wives head.

I really hope that Naomi is about to lose baby Angela, and that those six kids of Olivia's will be on the plane with the rest of the children.

Back in Canada, Moira and Luke are forced through TSA-like security so that Serena can see Nichole. I know it was part of getting Fred behind bars, but this seems awfully unfair.

Serena, with her hair down and in hip new clothes, looks 10

years younger. You can almost forget what a monster she really is. Luckily, Moira is there to remind her.

"Who the hell are you? You got some new clothes, but you're still the woman who held my friend down and raped her."

"That's uncalled for," Mark Truello breaks in.

"Fuck you," Moira tells him. Yeah. Fuck you Mark. Mark has had a hard on for Serena ever since he talked to her in that bar.

Anyway, as soon as Moira leaves, Nichole fusses and cries. The mandated social worker observing the visitation is giving her a hard time. You can tell Serena wants to go all Mrs. Waterford on her, but she gave that up for this child. I hope it was worth it. No, I don't. I hope Serena suffers. But for right now, I have to settle for her being inconvenienced.

Meanwhile, back in Gilead, Lawrence is screaming into the phone. The other Commanders want war with Canada and they want to close the border. That would certainly put a kink in their escape plans. Lawrence wants to move up the time frame, but June tells him that's impossible.

Eleanor wants to save all the children, and she's so far off her rocker that she wants to go door to door to get them all. June uses some tough love to convince Eleanor that she can't do that, that it would ruin their plans. Lawrence doesn't like June speaking to his wife that way, because as much of a prick that he is, he's very protective of Eleanor and loves her very much.

In Toronto, Mark is interrogating Fred, trying to get him to cut a deal for information about Gilead. Fred tells him that he's too smart to be manipulated and Mark gives up for the day, instead asking if he would speak to Luke Bankole.

Surprisingly, Fred agrees to talk to June's husband.

All Luke wants to know is why Fred could do things like this. Fred says he saves lives not, ruins them, and asks Luke why he did nothing when values plummeted and the birth rate was nonexistent.

Luke agrees that he did nothing, but "You're going to rot in here, knowing that your wife betrayed you."

"What about your wife?" Fred comes back with. Oh no, he didn't. You mean the wife you raped Fred?

"She'll come back to me," Luke tells him.

"Maybe," Fred says. "But the June Osborne you knew doesn't exist anymore. Gilead's changed her. I changed her."

187

I hate that he's right. I hate that he gets to sit there in a nice room, in a nice suit, drinking nice booze and be his smug, arrogant self. I hate that he got carte blanche to rape women, to use and discard them like they were nothing. His prison cell is more sumptuous than my first apartment. I want him to really and truly pay for his crimes.

Luckily, so does Luke. He gets in a solid punch before the guard pulls him off. It looked like it hurt too.

Back at the Lawrences, Eleanor has taken a lethal dose of sleeping pills and is slowly dying. June tries to wake her, but can't. She almost calls for help, but realizes that if she does it could endanger the mission. Lucid, Eleanor is at risk of running her mouth. Who knows what would happen in the hospital? So June makes the decision to just let her go. She kisses her on the forehead, leaves the tray in the hallway and waits for Sienna to discover Eleanor's dead body in the morning.

In Toronto, Serena is sleeping in a chair when Mark delivers a pizza and some reading material. It's almost like he's flirting with her. Yuck. She's a viper. Serena smiles when she realizes she can read and write again. All it cost her was her little finger and her useless husband.

The Lawrence household prepares for Eleanor's funeral and June tries to comfort him the best that she can. But he's bereft and heartbroken. At the gravesite, once everyone has left, Aunt Lydia allows June to go up to him, and they mourn Eleanor together. But there is something in his eyes when he looks at her. Could he possibly know she didn't try to save Eleanor? He could take his revenge and ruin everything.

I'm wondering if June will be placed in another household right away. She's got no reason to be there without his wife, and I'm not sure why she isn't immediately going back to the Red Center with Aunt Lydia.

Self-Care Suggestion:

Eleanor should have had a better life. She should have had access to the medications that she needed. There is no shame in needing medicine to be healthy. Take your medicine. If you haven't been prescribed any, take a daily vitamin and any supplements your doctor has approved. Don't struggle on without them. You're not weak or defective for needing medicine to survive or stay sane in this crazy world. You're a soldier, a fighter, and as one of the good people who need to watch out for encroaching evil, we need you at your best. Get a good night's sleep. Drink plenty of water. Get some exercise every day. Treat yourself with kindness and grace. You deserve it.

Chapter Thirty-Six: Under His Fucking Eye

Season Three, Episode Thirteen: Mayday

"I have made my decision."~Lawrence

*"It's not your decision. Men, fucking pathological. You are not in charge. **I am**. So go to your fucking office and find me a fucking map. Thank you."~June*

"This is still in my house! My house, young lady."~Lawrence

"You really think this is still your house?"~June

Trigger Warnings: Another harrowing escape attempt, shooting, flashback to pre-Gilead where women are treated like cattle and worse, brutality

Gut Punch Rating: 2—get the hankies out, but in a good way.

Favorite Quotes: "You said you weren't going to be any trouble." ~ Lawrence

"Yeah, I lied." ~ June

We see a bit of a flashback where unwomen—like mentally and physically handicapped people—are being carted off, probably to slaughter. Others are stripped naked, poked and prodded. Men are screaming at them to "shut the fuck up." Frightened and confused, the women are loaded through cattle carts, and cages, and put on a transport carrier into the unknown.

June talks about these ruthless men who were determined to subjugate her and the other women.

"It isn't about being right or having people or God on your side. In the end, victory goes to the one with the hardest heart."

As June walks back from Loaves and Fishes, the other

191

handmaids drop soap in her shopping bag. Today's the day and everyone is excited. June worries that this is a trap set by the Eyes, but she's willing to be ruthless and make it happen.

Aunt Lydia pulls June aside and tells her that the other girls look up to her, that she shouldn't do anything that would get them in trouble. I swear, Aunt Lydia has a nose for shit like this. She could put a serious cramp in the plan. I wonder if June will have to kill her too, to make this work.

I hope so.

"Watch yourself," Aunt Lydia warns.

"You got it," June replies. Under his fucking eye. I love that this was the last words they spoke to each other...or is it?

The household is preparing for their big night. Lawrence is planning on drawing security out of the neighborhood. Beth is freaking out and Sienna is demanding to help. Together, they're all going to make sure this works. They're packing water, bread, and food for the children. The soap is to rub on the gates so the hinges don't squeak and give them away. As June is out in the garden, she sees a Martha lurking with a pink clad girl.

She's early. She's way too fucking early. But June takes her in.

Back in Canada, Mark gives Serena a cup of coffee and tells her that she has meetings all day. She asks if she can decline any of them, but he says unfortunately she surrendered the right to do that.

"I didn't surrender my rights, I traded them for my daughter," Serena says, showing the vicious bitch side of her.

Mark gives her a day pass. Starting next week, she can leave the prison facility. She's in awe that she will be able to explore the city without an escort.

Yippee. Maybe she'll get hit by a bus.

Back in Gilead, June takes care of the little girl. She had walked all the way from Lexington and has a blister. The girl's name is Kiki and was set to be married off soon. She's 10.

"Will God still love me?" Kiki asks, when June tells her she's going to a place where she won't be forced to marry, where she can be whomever she wants to be, and wear whatever she likes.

"Yes," June says.

And that's why, when the Martha freaks out and wants to take the girl back home, June pulls a gun on her. The Martha gets away, but now June is on edge. Kiki's crying has her wheeling the gun on her instead, leading Beth to take Kiki back into the house, while June tries to keep her shit together.

Lawrence come in a bit later and tells her that the girl has to go back home to Lexington. There is a search going on and the guardians are going door-to-door looking for her. They'll be setting up roadblocks.

"I'm pulling the plug," Lawrence says.

June refuses to send Kiki back to be married off, to get raped and maimed. They'll find a way around the roadblocks. She orders Lawrence to find her a map.

Back in Toronto, Fred is singing like a canary.

"I have some uncomfortable information to depart... about my wife."

Mark tries to defend her as a victim of Gilead's law, but Fred is about to set him straight on just how powerless Serena really wasn't severed finger and all.

As the children pour into the Lawrence household, June and her crew decide that they'll walk to the airport to avoid the roadblocks, and set off to mark the trail themselves.

Meanwhile, Serena Joy's moment with Nichole comes to a very abrupt end as Mark storms into her visitation, telling the social worker to take the child. He charges Serena with sexual slavery, who counters that her plea agreement covers that, because Gilead forced her to do that under threat of execution. Except for that one time when she forced Nick and June to have sex.

"Nick and Offred had a relationship," Serena counters.

Offred?

Gotcha bitch.

"It's still rape, Mrs. Waterford," Mark says coldly.

Gee Serena, could this be what the other women felt when their children were torn from them, before they themselves were imprisoned?

Fred, you vindictive, devious bastard. The two of you deserve each other, but hopefully you'll never see each other or baby Nichole ever again.

Rot in prison, assholes.

Back in Gilead, all the lights are off at the Lawrence home. It doesn't look good. But June and the others walk in to hear Lawrence reading the children Robert Louis Stevenson's *Treasure Island*. And there's a lot more than 52 children.

Janine arrives with news. The guardians are on their way, looking for Kiki. Their time is running out. They have to take the children now.

June asks Lawrence to come with them, but he declines, saying that Eleanor would have liked him to stay and clean up his mess.

"God grant you peace, Joseph."

"And you, June Osborne."

They take the children through the woods, hiding from the guardians until they get to the airport. Luckily, Gilead has trained the kids to be quiet. June provides a distraction while Rita takes the children towards the plane.

Running through the woods, June gets shot and falls to the ground. But when the guard kicks her over, she has her gun drawn and forces him to call in the all clear. After he does, she shoots him and collapses. June lays on her back and watches the sky until the plane roars overhead.

When it lands in Canada, there are several American refugees volunteering. They don't know exactly what the cargo is, but they're prepared for everything. Moira and Emily are front and center, as is Luke.

When Kiki steps off the plane, a man immediately recognizes her. "Rebecca?" he says, as she runs into her Daddy's arms.

Oh, poor Luke, just waiting to see Hannah come down those stairs, only to watch the plane empty of other people's children.

Even Rita's words that June was the one who made this all happen isn't enough, but it is something.

Back in Gilead, June is wounded and maybe dying. But her friends, the other handmaids, carry her out of the forest like pallbearers while she dreams of Luke and Hannah on a beautiful day in the park.

Self-Care Suggestion:

A good cry might be in order.

After You've Watched

*"I have seen, I have seen the affliction of my people
which is in Egypt, and I have heard their groaning,
and am come down to deliver them.
And now come, I will send thee into Egypt."*
~Acts 7:34, King James Bible

I read the sequel to *The Handmaid's Tale, The Testaments*. No spoilers here except to say that it answered the questions I've been waiting almost 35 years for. And while I'm not completely overjoyed with the ending, I am satisfied with it. A piece of the puzzle that has been missing for me all those years is now snugly in place.

If you haven't read *The Testaments*, go read it now. Aunt Lydia is one of the point of view characters, and while I still have a lot of questions and I don't forgive her, she has her reasons. Also, she didn't become an Aunt because she wanted the "D" and didn't get it right away. I'm still pissed about that.

If I didn't know that there was a fourth season planned, I would be very happy with this ending, especially after having read *The Testaments*. If Hulu and the show runners decided to have Mayday be the series finale, it would have worked.

I do still have a few minor questions though. Was baby Angela on that plane? Did Fred and Serena suffer in prison? Did Emily and Sylvia make it work? But my imagination can come up with answers for those.

What I'm worried about is the fourth season. How can it tell June's story? Once Gilead wakes up the next morning, they will go to war with Canada. They were prepared to do it over Nichole, and losing over 52 children is going to have them turning the tanks and fighter jets to our neighbor in the North.

I'm not sure Toronto and the rest of Canada are ready for a full-fledged war. And what about June and the handmaids? There's a lot of executions coming down. I can't imagine Lawrence can keep them all from the wall.

Although, stranger things have happened. Maybe June will be given to a nice Commander that she can run roughshod over, or maybe she'll be given to a vicious one that will want to sew her lips shut. Or maybe she becomes a teal blue clad wife to Commander Blaine and together they take down Gilead from the inside.

Okay, I'd watch the hell out of that last one.

Lately, there's been some rumors that Season Four will take place 15 years later—which is about the time *The Testaments* takes place. I'd be all for that, especially with flashbacks of the ensuing years where I get all my questions answered.

While I'm curious to see what happens next season, I'm glad for the break. This is not an easy series to binge watch, and if you've stayed with me this long, I want to thank you. I'm humbled and honored you took this journey with me.

Please though, if you are haunted by the themes and the images in this show, talk to a qualified professional. If you've experienced rape or abuse, PTSD is very common and there are people who want to help you, and can help you. If you are bipolar, like Eleanor Lawrence, there is help available. Please reach out for medical assistance.

And for those of us who can still see Gilead looming over our horizon, even with (as of this writing) Trump waning in power and all of us still being quarantined by Covid-19, there is hope. World leaders like Canada's Justin Trudeau, Germany's Angela Merkel, New Zealand's Prime Minister, Jacinda Ardem, and even England's Queen Elizabeth will provide a light in the darkness. But even during this dark time in the United States, we have our own squad: Alexandria Ocasio-Cortez of New York, Ilhan Omar of Minnesota, Ayanna Pressley of Massachusetts, and Rashida Tlaib of Michigan. There's also Stacey Abrams whose work in Georgia was invaluable to the 2020 election. And if all goes well, Dr. Jill Biden and Vice President-elect Kamala Harris will be in the White House. An end, hopefully, is in sight, hopefully January 20, 2021.

But even if it isn't, we can stop Gilead from happening. Don't stop protesting. Don't stop writing your Representatives, and Congressmen and women. Don't allow yourself to step on others to climb up the social or economical ladder.

We are all in this together. Yes, smash the patriarchy, but also support all women, no matter what their race, religion, or sexuality is. In fact, embrace kindness to all genders and don't accept racism or sexism. People will make mistakes. We need to educate and lift each other up with respect and love.

We will be the light in the darkness.

I tell my son every day to **think** before he speaks.

> T = True
> H = Helpful
> I = Inspiring
> N = Necessary
> K = Kind

If it's not, don't say it. But most of all, I want him to think. Social media and the internet are both a blessing and a curse. One of my favorite memes comes from a Reddit feed:

"If someone in the 1950s suddenly appeared today, what would be the most difficult thing to explain to them about life today?"

"I possess a device in my pocket that is capable of accessing the entirety of information known to man. I use it to look at pictures of cats and get into arguments with strangers."

We all need to be well read and to check our sources, because there's a lot of propaganda out there that wants to separate us from each other. United we stand, divided we fall. We're not always going to agree with each other, and there are some pretty evil people out there, but I firmly believe there are more good guys than bad guys. We outnumber them. We have more in common with each other than we think. Once we connect, they can't tear us apart. Only we can tear us apart.

Help people when you can. Accept help when you need it. We'll get through this. We will persevere. Gilead will always fail in the end because of good people willing to speak out.

Speak out.

Get loud.

Read.

And above all:

Nolite te bastardes carborundorum

Bibliography

https://www.imdb.com/
https://en.wikipedia.org/

Works Cited

Grady, C. (2019, May 2). *Vox*. Retrieved from Vox.com: https://www.vox.com/culture/2019/5/2/18524155/avengers-endgame-failed-black-widow

James, K. (2020). *King James Bible Online*. Retrieved from King James Bible Online.org: https://www.kingjamesbibleonline.org/Genesis-Chapter-30/

Lawler, K. (2017, April 20). *USA Today*. Retrieved from USAToday.com: https://www.usatoday.com/story/life/entertainthis/2017/04/20/elisabeth-moss-dont-binge-the-handmaids-tale-hulu-margaret-atwood

Graham, Ruth and LaFraniere, Sharon (2020, October 22). The New York Times. Retrieved from NYtimes.com: https://www.nytimes.com/2020/10/08/us/people-of-praise-amy-coney-barrett.html

About the Author

USA Today bestselling author, Jamie K. Schmidt is known for her erotically charged romances, Jamie's books have been called, "hot and sexy, with just the right amount of emotional punch," and "turbo-paced, gritty, highly sexual thrill rides." As a #1 Amazon best seller and a 2018 Romance Writers of America Rita® finalist in erotica, Jamie writes daily, drinks lots of tea, and sneaks away to play World of Warcraft whenever she makes her deadlines. Along with her husband who lets her stick magnetic signs on his car about her books and her 12-year-old son who wants to be her cover model, Jamie lives in Connecticut with her rescue pup Romeo, who is cool with her writing schedule as long as he can be cuddled up in a blanket next to her. You can find Jamie on Twitter at @jamiekswriter and on Facebook at jamie.k.schmidt.1, where she'll be chatting about her latest book and wishing desperately for a kitten to be her new writing buddy and some carbs—not necessarily in that order.

Other Riverdale Avenue Books You Might Like

The Binge Watcher's Guide to Doctor Who:
A History of the Doctor Who and the First Female Doctor
By Mackenzie Flohr

The Binge Watcher's Guide to the Films of Harry Potter
An Unauthorized Guide
By Cecilia Tan

1984 in the 21st Century:
An Anthology of Essays
Edited by Lori Perkins'

Everything You Always Wanted to Know about Watergate*
*But Were Afraid to Ask
By Brian O'Connor and Lori Perkins

If you liked this book,
Please join our mailing list at RiverdaleAveBooks.com